LIGHT IN THE EAST

TimeFrame AD 1000-1100

KIEVAN RUSSIA

EUROPE: THE NORMANS

THE MIDDLE EAST

TimeFrame AD 1000-1100

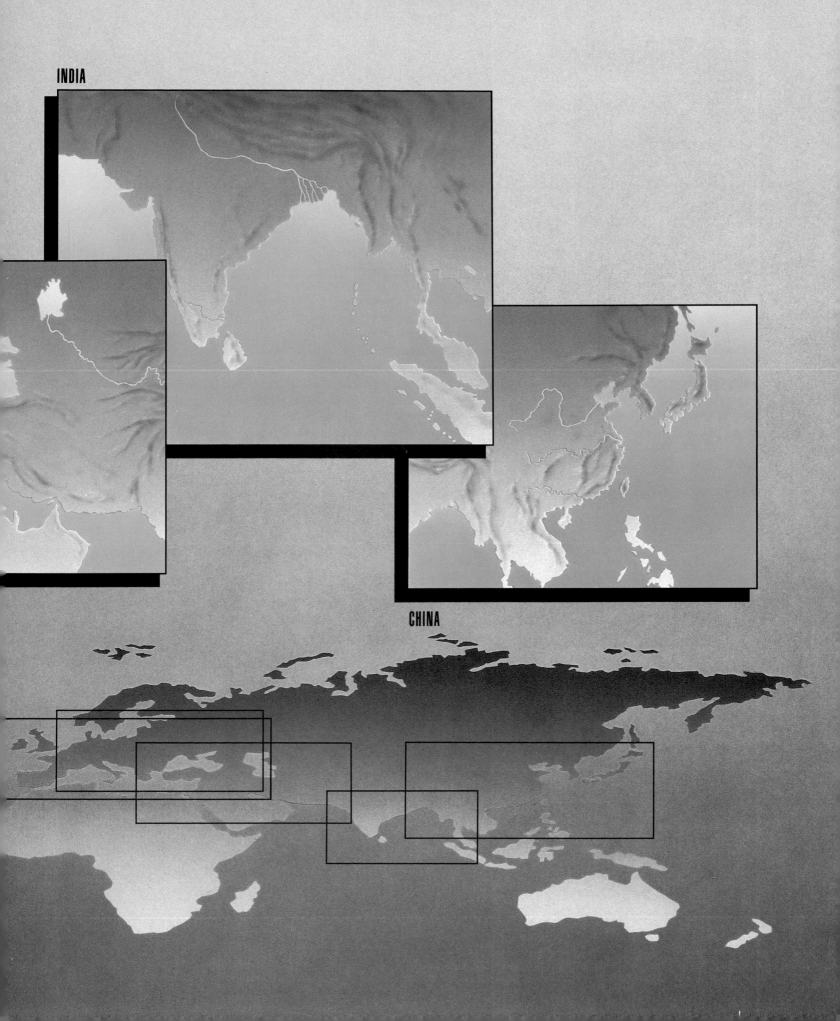

INDIA

CHINA

TIME®
LIFE
BOOKS

Other Publications:
THE TIME-LIFE GARDENER'S GUIDE
MYSTERIES OF THE UNKNOWN
FIX IT YOURSELF
FITNESS, HEALTH & NUTRITION
SUCCESSFUL PARENTING
HEALTHY HOME COOKING
UNDERSTANDING COMPUTERS
LIBRARY OF NATIONS
THE ENCHANTED WORLD
THE KODAK LIBRARY OF CREATIVE PHOTOGRAPHY
GREAT MEALS IN MINUTES
THE CIVIL WAR
PLANET EARTH
COLLECTOR'S LIBRARY OF THE CIVIL WAR
THE EPIC OF FLIGHT
THE GOOD COOK
WORLD WAR II
HOME REPAIR AND IMPROVEMENT
THE OLD WEST

For information on and a full description of
any of the Time-Life Books series listed above,
please call 1-800-621-7026 or write:
Reader Information
Time-Life Customer Service
P.O. Box C-32068
Richmond, Virginia 23261-2068

LIGHT IN THE EAST

TimeFrame AD 1000-1100

BY THE EDITORS OF TIME-LIFE BOOKS

TIME-LIFE BOOKS, ALEXANDRIA, VIRGINIA

Time-Life Books Inc.
is a wholly owned subsidary of
TIME INCORPORATED

FOUNDER: Henry R. Luce 1898-1967

Editor-in-Chief: Jason McManus
Chairman and Chief Executive Officer:
J. Richard Munro
President and Chief Operating Officer:
N. J. Nicholas, Jr.
Editorial Director: Ray Cave
Executive Vice President, Books:
Kelso F. Sutton
Vice President, Books: George Artandi

TIME-LIFE BOOKS INC.

EDITOR: George Constable
Executive Editor: Ellen Phillips
Director of Design: Louis Klein
Director of Editorial Resources:
Phyllis K. Wise
Editorial Board: Russell B. Adams, Jr.,
Dale M. Brown, Roberta Conlan,
Thomas H. Flaherty, Lee Hassig, Donia
Ann Steele, Rosalind Stubenberg
Director of Photography and Research:
John Conrad Weiser
Assistant Director of Editorial Resources:
Elise Ritter Gibson

EUROPEAN EDITOR: Kit van Tulleken
Assistant European Editor: Gillian Moore
Design Director: Ed Skyner
Assistant Design Director: Mary Staples
Chief of Research: Vanessa Kramer
Chief Sub-Editor: Ilse Gray

PRESIDENT: Christopher T. Linen
Chief Operating Officer: John M. Fahey, Jr.
Senior Vice Presidents: Robert M.
DeSena, James L. Mercer, Paul R.
Stewart
Vice Presidents: Stephen L. Bair, Ralph J.
Cuomo, Neal Goff, Stephen L. Goldstein,
Juanita T. James, Hallett Johnson III,
Carol Kaplan, Susan J. Maruyama,
Robert H. Smith, Joseph J. Ward
Director of Production Services:
Robert J. Passantino

Correspondents: Elisabeth Kraemer-Singh
(Bonn); Maria Vincenza Aloisi (Paris);
Ann Natanson (Rome).

TIME FRAME
(published in Britain as
TIME-LIFE HISTORY OF THE WORLD)

SERIES EDITOR: Tony Allan

Editorial Staff for *Light in the East:*
Designer: Mary Staples
Writer: Christopher Farman
Researcher: Lesley Coleman
Sub-Editor: Diana Hill
Design Assistant: Rachel Gibson
Editorial Assistant: Molly Sutherland
Picture Department: Patricia Murray
(administrator), Amanda Hindley (picture
coordinator)

Editorial Production
Chief: Maureen Kelly
Production Assistant: Samantha Hill
Editorial Department: Theresa John,
Debra Lelliott

U.S. EDITION

Assistant Editor: Barbara Fairchild
Quarmby
Copy Coordinator: Jarelle S. Stein
Picture Coordinator: Robert H.
Wooldridge, Jr.

Editorial Operations
Copy Chief: Diane Ullius
Production: Celia Beattie
Library: Louise D. Forstall

Special Contributors: Windsor Chorlton,
John Cottrell, Alan Lothian, Robin Olson
(text); Caroline Alcock, Timothy Fraser,
Caroline Lucas, Linda Proud (research);
Roy Nanovic (index)

CONSULTANTS

China:
DENIS TWITCHETT, Gordon Wu Professor of Chinese Studies, Princeton University, Princeton, New Jersey

General:
GEOFFREY PARKER, Professor of Histo-
ry, University of Illinois,
Urbana-Champaign, Illinois

India:
C. A. BAYLY, Reader in Modern Indian
History, St. Catharine's College, Cam-
bridge University, Cambridge, England

Kievan Russia:
R. E. F. SMITH, Fellow of the Institute for
Advanced Research in the Humanities,
University of Birmingham, Birmingham,
England

Middle East:
ROBERT IRWIN, Visiting lecturer in me-
dieval history at Oxford University, Ox-
ford, England; Cambridge University,
Cambridge, England; University of Lon-
don, London, England; University of St.
Andrews, Fife, Scotland; and author of
The Middle East in the Middle Ages

PETER SLUGLETT, Lecturer in Modern
Middle Eastern History, Durham University, Durham, England

Western Europe:
CHRISTOPHER GIVEN-WILSON, Lectur-
er in Medieval History, University of St.
Andrews, Fife, Scotland

DAVID NICOLLE, Author of *Arms and
Armor of the Crusading Era, 1050-1350*

**Library of Congress Cataloging in
Publication Data**

Light in the East: time frame AD 1000-1100 /
by the editors of Time-Life Books.
p.   cm. — (Time frame)
Bibliography: p.
Includes index.
ISBN 0-8094-6429-2.
ISBN 0-8094-6430-6 (lib. bdg.).
1. Eleventh century.
I. Time-Life Books. II. Series.
D201.4.L54 1988
909'.1—dc19   88-24926 CIP

Time-Life Books Inc. offers a wide range of fine
recordings, including a *Rock 'n' Roll Era* series.
For subscription information, call 1-800-621-
7026 or write Time-Life Music, P.O. Box C-
32068, Richmond, Virginia 23261-2068.

CONTENTS

CHINA'S ENLIGHTENED EMPIRE

1 Had a traveler from western Europe been able to visit Kaifeng, capital of Song China in the eleventh century, he would have been amazed by what he saw. In place of the rural world of illiterate barons and peasants with which he was familiar, he would have found an open city of broad streets, wide canals, and many trees, crowded with a shifting population of merchants, voyagers, government officials, and workers. Stalls overflowing with merchandise lined its avenues. Markets opened at dawn and closed after midnight. Vendors, hawking everything from toys and sweetmeats to horoscopes and hot water, vied for shoppers' attention, while signboards advertised all sorts of goods and services. Even professionals marketed their skills vigorously: "Rapid Recovery Assured," promised one sign outside a doctor's office.

It was a convivial city, whose architecture reflected its lively street life. Shop fronts stood wide open to passersby, while taverns and restaurants offered pavement tables and benches. The wooden-framed houses were more window than wall, with screens of bamboo latticework letting in the sun and the street noise. Balconies and porches overlooked courtyards and thoroughfares. Tier upon tier of upturned tile roofs made an undulating skyline, broken regularly by watchtowers that gave firefighters a view across a panorama of potential kindling in a city built largely of wood. Above them all rose tall pagodas, topped with yellow tiles.

The citizenry mingled not only in the shops and streets, but in vast, tented pleasure grounds that provided a platform for entertainers of all kinds—acrobats, jugglers, puppeteers, musicians, storytellers, and comedians. Eating places were everywhere: Citizens could dine in cheap little noodle shops or in grand restaurants with more than 100 rooms, where patrons could choose from extensive menus of local specialties or dishes from other regions. Smoked oranges, baby fish, hundred-flavors soup, lamb steamed over milk—choice meals were always available.

Such opulence and display were rare commodities indeed in the eleventh century, which for most people in Europe and elsewhere was far from being an age of plenty. Yet for all its harshness it was, in contrast to the two centuries that preceded it, a time of fresh hopes and beginnings. The benefits were not at once apparent, for the dominant figure in most lands other than China was still the warrior subjugating less powerful beings by naked force. But ravagers who in the past had been content to plunder, kill, and then move on now chose to settle. The rule of these mighty warlords was fierce; but it provided the order under which the seeds of economic and cultural development could germinate.

Around the world, the century started unpropitiously. Western Europe had for 200 years been subject to the depredations of Viking marauders sweeping down from the north, Magyars raiding from the east, and the forces of Islam, who mounted their challenge from the lands they held in Spain and North Africa. In the face of this

This porcelain beast, part lion and part dog, once guarded a Buddhist shrine in Song China, where, seated on a pillar, it served to scare off demons. Lions were not native to the country, but they have always featured prominently in Chinese legends. According to one, the lion could produce milk from its paws; receptacles such as the hollow ball shown here would have served to collect the liquid.

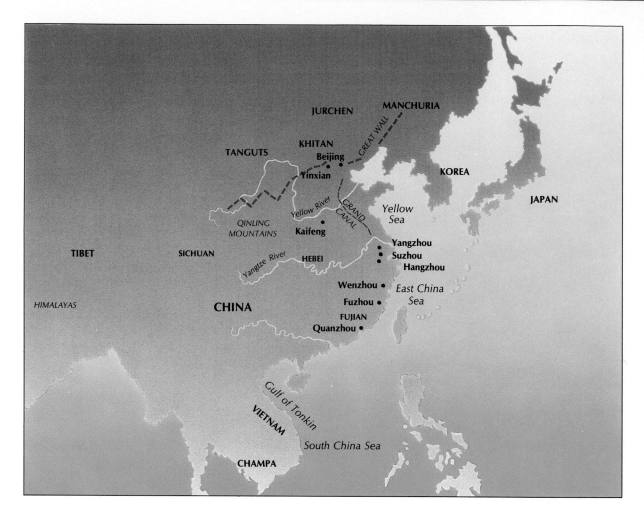

three-pronged assault, society had disintegrated into its smallest constituent parts: People had turned to the local baron for protection on whatever terms it was offered, and feudalism in its harshest and most primitive form had been born. The Islamic lands had also seen a weakening of central authority as the great Abbasid caliphate of Harun al-Rashid had collapsed into a congeries of semi-independent local dynasties, leaving the rulers of Baghdad with no more than a nominal headship over their former provinces. To the east, China had experienced the final breakup of its great Tang civilization, and India, though economically and culturally advanced, remained politically divided. Of all the great powers of the day, only Byzantium had survived and flourished within its eastern Mediterranean heartlands.

By the year 1000, however, the situation was changing. In Europe, the Arab threat had been contained, and the Magyars, defeated by the German emperor at the Lechfeld in 955, had settled in Hungary to a sedentary life. The Vikings too were putting down roots in some of the lands they had earlier pillaged. Some, who had made their home in northern France, took the name of Normans. Swapping their longboats for horses, armor, and lances, they were to become the most formidable military force in eleventh-century Europe. Another group, known as the Rus, drawn from the ranks of Vikings who traded down the river system between the Baltic and the Black Sea, had won themselves a kingdom based in the city of Kiev. The composite realm they created, part Viking and part Slav, was to bear the name of Russia.

New forces made their influence felt in the Islamic world as well. In the course of the century, Islam experienced the irruption of a horse-riding warrior people whose influence was to be even more profound than that of the Normans on Europe. At the start of the century, the Seljuk Turks were an undistinguished border tribe, recently converted to Islam; by 1054, however, they had already become the masters of Baghdad, and under the peace they imposed, the lands of the Middle East were to enter a new era of order and comparative unity. Meanwhile in southern India, beyond the farthermost reaches of Islam, a Hindu empire was established by two great warrior-kings of the Chola people.

No other land, however, blossomed as China did. The fifty-year time of troubles that followed the final extinction of the Tang dynasty did relatively little damage to the infrastructure of the nation's life. Once firm central rule was reestablished by the Song emperors from 960 on, peace and prosperity were quickly restored. With a swiftly growing population flowing into cities and towns, a booming economy, and a government administered by a professional bureaucracy, Song China led the world in refinement and civilization.

China's development under the Song was remarkable. From 60 million inhabitants when the dynasty arose, the population surged toward the 100 million mark by the year 1100. As the populace grew it became more commercial and more urban. Literacy and learning offered advancement, and social mobility became more possible as the old military aristocracy gave way to a ruling elite of educated civil servants whose ranks were open to all through competitive examinations. At the highest level, these bureaucrats ruled under emperors who largely allowed their ministers to set national policy.

For a century and a half, Song China prospered under an orderly succession of eight consecutive emperors. Then disaster struck; the last of the eight, Huizong, lost his throne to invaders from the north. Kaifeng, together with about a third of the empire's lands, fell to the attackers before a son of Huizong managed to reestablish imperial rule from a new capital at Hangzhou, almost 470 miles to the southeast. He and his successors became known as the Southern Song emperors, to distinguish them from their predecessors of the Song dynasty proper, ruling from Kaifeng.

Like most of China's great dynasties, the Song owed its creation to a military coup. The imperial army based around Kaifeng revolted against the last emperor of the preceding Zhou dynasty and offered the throne instead to its commanding officer, General Zhao Kuangyin. Zhao accepted the offer, on condition that the life of the emperor be spared, and acceded to the throne under the name of Taizu.

In so doing, he took up an imperial inheritance that already stretched back more than a millennium, to the third century BC, when the first emperor of the Qin dynasty had united feudal China under his rule. In the succeeding centuries, Chinese history followed a cyclical pattern: Eras of strong, centralized rule under such dynasties as the Han and the Tang alternated with periods of strife, when the country would break up into a confusing collection of warring states.

The Chinese were, then, well aware of the need for firm government, but the tendency toward autocracy was tempered by a sense of the responsibilities of power. The emperor's authority to rule was, by common consent, God-given, but not irre-

China under the Song dynasty stretched from the mountains of western Sichuan to the East China Sea. In the north, its frontier fell short of the 1,200-year-old Great Wall, which had been breached by the Khitan, a people of Mongolian stock, in the century before; the invaders subsequently established one of their capitals at Beijing. In the south, the Vietnamese territories held in earlier days had also been lost in the time of troubles following the downfall of the preceding Tang dynasty.

In the early Song years, the heart of the nation was the Yellow River and its surrounding lands; but in the course of the eleventh century, the focus of commerce and population shifted southward to the fertile Yangtze Valley and the southeast.

versible. The Chinese believed that their rulers reigned by the mandate of heaven: Divine will placed an individual on the throne but could remove him, too, if he failed to govern well. For the concept of good government was as ancient as the imperial tradition itself—every dynasty since the Qin had included officials charged with routing corruption both from the bureaucracy at large and from the palace itself. Of course, such safeguards were not infallible, but their very existence testified to an ingrained regard for the obligation to rule well.

Social responsibility and a concern for popular welfare were central concerns of the philosophy of Confucius, whose ethical and political teachings, promulgated in the sixth century BC, had influenced official attitudes since the earliest days of imperial rule. Living in a time of war and discord, Confucius preached the virtues of harmony. In social terms, that meant an ordered hierarchy in which each individual had his or her place; those above had a duty to govern wisely and foster the welfare of their subjects, while those below were expected to accept their condition. By Song times, Confucian precepts were deeply entrenched in the Chinese way of thinking.

Confucianism was not, however, the nation's only ideology; other, more spiritual, doctrines were also widely held. Daoism, born in China in the fourth century BC, drew widespread support for its mystical message advocating withdrawal from worldly concerns and communion with nature; the Buddhist faith, preaching the virtues of contemplation and self-purification, arrived from India two centuries later and also grew in popularity over the intervening centuries. Buddhism in particular became so prevalent and drew so many people away from productive society into the cloister that the Tang government attempted to suppress it in the ninth century. By the time of Taizu's accession, it had partially revived, however, and all three belief systems were to coexist under the Song, with many people following an amalgam of practices and ideas from all of them.

The most pressing task facing the new ruler was the need to reunite his divided country. He was helped in these efforts by the war-weariness that inevitably followed fifty years of civil strife. Using a combination of tact, military strength, and bribery, Taizu persuaded the warlords who dominated the other northern states to accept his rule, in return for wealthy sinecures and honorary titles. After establishing a tightly centralized government in the northern lands, he next launched a series of campaigns to regain southern territories held by local regimes. (Reunification would be completed by the dynasty's second emperor in 979.)

Taizu's next priority was to reduce the power of the army commanders, proven troublemakers of the recent past. As he himself reportedly said, he could not sleep peacefully at night for the thought that the emperor's yellow robe might one day be placed on one of his old comrades as it had been on him. His solution to the problem was to weaken the power base of individual commanders and at the same time to place the army as a whole firmly under civilian control. In pursuit of the former goal, he took care to divide the palace armies—the bulk of the armed forces, including their crack troops, based in the Kaifeng region—into three separate divisions, whose commanders each reported directly to the emperor. He also limited the tours of duty of units dispatched to the borders to three years, thereby fixing the soldiers' loyalty to their Kaifeng base rather than to local commanders. To supervise the running of the army as a whole, he set up a Bureau of Military Affairs, staffed by civilian administrators. Under Taizu and his successors, the ranks were formed of professional soldiers owing their allegiance to the emperor alone.

Taizu, portrayed here as a benign father figure by an unknown court painter, was the first emperor of the Song dynasty. Seizing power in 960, he took over a country still divided into several independent states. Over the next sixteen years, he used tactful diplomacy and military force to reunite the nation and to bring the army to heel. He was a formidable general whose victories restored central control over territories lost to local warlords; he was also a wise administrator whose reforms ushered in an era of stability.

The land that the army protected was smaller than it had been in the past. At its greatest extent under the Han, who ruled at the start of the Christian era, China had included all the territory between present-day North Korea and coastal Vietnam; the Great Wall, snaking 1,500 miles from the Yellow Sea to the deserts of Turkestan, protected it from the nomadic peoples to the north, while to the west the realm rose up to the mountains of western Sichuan. Rarely, though, in succeeding centuries had the imperial writ run that far; in times of weak central power, the high plateaus to the west of the mountains provided shelter for independent kingdoms often fiercely hostile to the emperors, while the northern nomads, cousins of the Huns and the Mongols, would take advantage of the situation to penetrate the Wall.

Such was the case under the Song. In the south, the emperors' authority no longer reached the Gulf of Tonkin, for the lands composing present-day Vietnam had gained independence during the time of troubles following the fall of the Tang. In the north, Song power stopped well short of the Great Wall. The Khitan, a race of horse-riding warriors related to the Mongols, had in the previous century built up a powerful empire that straddled that barrier, including the region around the city of Beijing. Adjoining the Khitan territories to the west, a second hostile empire developed in the course of the eleventh century. The Tanguts, a federation of Tibetan tribes, won control of the high plateau beyond China's northwestern border, lands that included the eastern end of the Silk Road, northern China's main trade route to the Middle East.

Although the Chinese dismissed both the Tanguts and the Khitan as barbarians, they were in fact formidable powers, probably more populous, and certainly bigger, than any contemporary European nation. They were better administered too, being organized along semi-Chinese lines by educated elites. Throughout the century, these states stood poised to strike at the Song.

The rulers of eleventh-century China dealt with the threat to their northern borders by buying off the enemy, but the price they had to pay was high. The third Song emperor agreed by treaty to pay annual subsidies to the Khitan in 1004; from 1044, the Tanguts benefited from a similar arrangement. Measured out in silk and silver delivered into foreign treasuries, these indemnities never amounted to more than 2 percent of Song revenues; but they placed China in a position of obligation to neighbors who continued to harass the nation with occasional border skirmishes and demands for higher payment.

Yet throughout the century, from the Great Wall in the north and the Tibetan foothills in the west to the South and East China seas, the empire remained whole. Sprawling across more than 965,000 square miles, it stretched from the harsh flood plain of the temperamental Yellow River in the north, over the spine of the Qinling Mountains, to a lush south watered by the many-armed Yangtze. A network of roads, canals, lakes, and rivers spanned its territories, and the traders who plied it spun a web of commerce that linked spice growers of the southwest with silk weavers in the northeast, and papermakers in Sichuan with copper miners in Fujian. As the years of peace unfolded, the thriving trade industry, as much as political stability, held Chinese society together.

"In the north, take a horse; in the south, take a boat" was ancient advice to Chinese travelers, and eleventh-century traders still followed it. Navigable rivers were comparatively few in the north and the roads—many newly paved in stone or brick—teemed with horsemen, oxcarts, high officials and their ladies carried aloft in litters on the shoulders of sweating servants, and peasants on foot shouldering bamboo poles strung with bundles. A great canal carried goods between the capital of Kaifeng, on the Yellow River, and the southern provinces, where trade was waterborne. Southern commerce flowed along a system of linked rivers, lakes, creeks, even irrigation ditches. So extensive was this system that the master of a river vessel could chart a continuous voyage of thousands of miles entirely on the inland waterways.

Many shipyards were active in the eleventh century, and China's waters were busy. Vessels skimmed along under sails of reed or bamboo matting. Others were swept forward by the graceful swish of fishtail-shaped oars. In shallow waters, boats were punted by pole-wielding crews that could number in the dozens, while in deep harbors, human-powered paddle wheelers served as tugs. At whitewater stretches on the rivers, boats were hauled over rapids by water buffalo turning capstans on shore. Swift naval vessels with elegant, low-prowed profiles shared the waterways with floating cities of homely houseboats crowded with families.

At the heart of the communications network was Kaifeng, seat of government and of the imperial court, which blossomed under the reign of Taizu and his successors. At the start of the Song period, it was an orderly administrators' city, carefully planned in districts, with different trades confined by law to specific neighborhoods. The whole was protected by an encircling outer wall. In the course of the century, though, the population spilled out several times over a succession of ever-larger ramparts, creating teeming suburbs beyond the massive city gates. Meanwhile, the designated mercantile districts also burst their bounds under commercial pressure, and stores, stalls, studios, and workshops opened all over the city.

A similar pattern of urban growth repeated itself elsewhere in the country, as peasants left the land to seek new opportunities in the cities. Eleventh-century China had ten cities that—together with their surrounding districts—numbered more than a million inhabitants. Some, such as Yangzhou and Suzhou, were in the Chinese economic heartland around the Yangtze River; but other towns grew up in the previously underpopulated northern frontier zone. The most dramatic growth came in the south, where port cities—including Hangzhou, Wenzhou, and Quanzhou—mushroomed in size in response to the profits of a growing ocean trade. To their wharves came gold and pearls from Japan, spices and ivory from Southeast Asia, in exchange for the silks and lacquer ware, the porcelain and bronzes that were to carry the reputation of Chinese luxury goods around the world.

One precondition for the expansion of sea trade under the Song was improved ship design. Great multidecked junks appeared, equipped with such innovations as steering rudders, stabilizing outriggers, and mariners' compasses. Although south-pointing magnetic compasses had been used earlier by Daoist geomancers to determine the proper siting of religious rituals, eleventh-century sailors began to navigate with them and were thus able to open trade routes to lands as far away as India's Malabar Coast and the Persian Gulf.

Supplied with the fruits of foreign trade as well as internal production, Song trade routes bustled with commerce. A nationwide market existed for many products, especially rice. Of all the vessels plowing Chinese waters, the big flat-bottomed rice boats were by far the most numerous; harvest time drew them in such dense fleets that, in the eyes of one observer, the rivers themselves seemed to vanish beneath the crush of vessels. The government taxed output to build up vast official stores of grain, which were used to feed the army, relieve famine, and stabilize market supply and prices. Grain sold commercially passed from the rice paddy to the cooking pot

A City at Work and Play

Located in the Yellow River valley at the heart of the productive North China plain, Kaifeng, the Song capital, was a bustling metropolis of almost a million people. Its canals were thronged with barges carrying rice, wood, coal, bricks, tiles, and salt; its narrow streets were busy with craft workshops; pottery kilns and iron foundries flourished on the outskirts. But pleasure was no less important than work to its citizens; the town was renowned for its sophisticated cuisine and its many theaters.

Its streets were at their busiest for the springtime festival of Qing Ming, literally "pure and bright," when citizens left their homes and journeyed out into the countryside to clean the tombs of their ancestors. All the bustle of this convivial season is captured in an extraordinary scroll executed in the late eleventh or early twelfth century by a court painter called Zhang Zeduan. More than sixteen feet long, the work presents a pageant of urban life in a time of peace and prosperity.

Tradition records that the painting once belonged to the last emperor of the Song dynasty proper. In his reign, Jurchen tribesmen invaded China from Manchuria, seizing the capital along with about one-third of the nation's land. Thereafter, the city remained an important administrative center, but its days of cultural and commercial preeminence were gone forever.

A detail from Zhang Zeduan's scroll painting *Going Upriver at the Qing Ming Festival* shows onlookers watching a grain boat negotiate a wooden bridge in the Song capital of Kaifeng.

At a busy crossroads in the capital, donkey carts and porters carrying goods strung from bamboo poles vie for space with strolling pedestrians and rich men carried in sedan chairs. At one corner of the intersection, a professional storyteller entertains passersby. Street stalls offer such snacks as soup, steamed cakes, and rice gruel, while more elaborate fare is served at the three-story restaurant *(top right)*.

A train of camels burdened with local produce leaves the Song capital through one of its twelve main gates, which is surmounted by an ornate guardhouse. Within the walls, commerce flourishes: A public scribe writes letters for a fee, while a prospective client tests the suppleness of a bow offered for sale by an archery dealer. In the center foreground a barber shaves a customer.

through an array of middlemen—warehousers who stored it, merchants who shipped it, brokers who bought it at the market, and shopkeepers who sold it to the consumers.

It took a growing abundance of rice to fuel this vigorous trade. After a devastating famine in the year 1012, the government imported a new, superior strain of rice from Champa—present-day southern Vietnam. The drought-resistant Champa rice ripened so quickly that two crops could be harvested each year, and the authorities sent agricultural experts throughout the rice-growing regions to distribute the new seed. Agricultural advisers also handed out pamphlets illustrating improved irrigation techniques, explaining the use of human waste for fertilizer, and recommending new kinds of farm equipment such as plows and harrows of improved design. Yields soared and the amount of land under cultivation doubled.

There was wide trading in many other agricultural products—such fruits as litchis, plums, loquats, oranges, and apricots, every sort of vegetable from leeks and turnips to eggplants and garlic, as well as cattle, pigs, and commercially reared fish. Cane sugar was refined and sold throughout the land in powdered, granulated, and lump form. Merchants dealt in countless varieties of oil, among them tung (made from tung-tree seeds) for boatbuilding, hemp (from the hemp plant) for lamps, perilla (from the perilla mint) for waterproofing silk rainwear, and burweed for treating colds.

The growing Song population needed great quantities of wood, both for fuel and for building ships and houses. A nationwide timber market developed, involving logging, lumber transport, and the first commercial tree farms. There was also a heavy demand for cryptomeria, used to make coffins. The wood fetched such a high price that, when daughters were born, farsighted fathers planted seedlings with the aim of providing dowries when both girls and trees were grown.

Heavy industries were booming, with iron and steel output on the rise to meet the need for metal goods, from swords to plowshares. These were large-scale industries; a single ironworks in the northwestern region of Hobei, for example, employed nearly 3,000 people. National iron output reached a record annual total of 137,500 long tons before the century was out.

Another popular commodity both for export and domestic use was paper, which was made by pounding and macerating bamboo shoots, vines, or mulberry-tree bark, then drying the resulting pulp on screens of various shapes and sizes. Fine, expensive papers had long been used by the elite, who could afford them, but the poor grades, made from insufficiently pulped materials, had been unsatisfactory; at the start of the century, one scholar complained that his legal notes disintegrated before the cases he was recording were decided. Over the decades, however, quality improved, and bamboo and mulberry-bark papers were widely produced for the mass market in many different colors, finishes, and thicknesses. The finest quality was used by artists and officials, while the cheapest was made into toilet paper or the imitation money that popular convention demanded should be burned in sacrifices to the gods.

Although barter was still widespread and many taxes were paid in kind, real money was increasingly essential to the economy. Copper currency, which under previous dynasties had been minted only in small quantities, now came to dominate the marketplace. By mid-century, imperial revenues in coin for the first time exceeded revenues in goods, and the government was soon issuing twenty times as much money each year as the Tang dynasty mints had. The coins, each worth about a thirtieth of a gram of silver, were pierced with a hole, through which they could be strung together, and stamped with the legend "Circulating Treasure of Song." The currency remained an unwieldy means of barter, since the official unit of exchange was a string of one thousand coins weighing almost one and a half pounds. Nonetheless, the demand was such that China's copper reserves were seriously depleted.

Instruments of credit supplemented the cash supply. Merchants placed coins in deposit houses and used the receipts as security for far-flung commercial transactions. In addition, the bureaus in charge of such government monopolies as salt and tea issued transferable exchange certificates, which could be redeemed in either cash or commodities, and a specially appointed agency printed several denominations of notes secured by a cash reserve: the world's first paper currency.

Regulating the money supply, levying taxes, influencing the grain market, and controlling monopolies in several commodities, the state kept a firm hand on the economy and on the country as a whole. Its agents were the thousands of officials who administered local, regional, and national affairs and who together made up the huge bureaucracy that extended the imperial government's reach into every corner of China and into most aspects of Chinese life.

The civil service drew its personnel from the ranks of the new educated class that had supplanted the military aristocracy as China's governing elite. At a time when the rulers of most European nations were still illiterate, China's educational system was geared to produce a meritocracy of talent, thoroughly versed in centuries of the nation's culture. Song civil servants owed their advancement more to success in competitive examinations and good job-performance reviews by their superiors than to family wealth or rank.

The system was not entirely egalitarian; young men of the upper classes had more time to immerse themselves in study than their laboring peasant counterparts, and so a majority of administrators were wellborn. Yet the establishment of publicly funded schools to recruit students from a wider field made the bureaucracy more open to talented newcomers than ever before. Some 40 percent of leading officials in the eleventh century were the sons of obscure families. All of them, however, were holders of prestigious doctoral degrees, without which even the scions of prominent families could not hope for preferment to high office.

The road to academic success was arduous. The curriculum was narrow, being focused entirely on the ancient canon of philosophical and literary works, supplemented by officially approved commentaries on the same texts. Students memorized precepts and debated interpretations, while candidates for examinations polished their skills of prose and poetry composition in the traditional styles. The aim was in all cases the same: the absorption, expression, and application of Confucian philosophy, with its message of moral and social order.

As soon as they had mastered basic reading skills (generally around the age of ten), pupils began to study the Confucian texts in their local schools. These institutions were operated throughout the empire by district or prefectural governments, some in specially built premises, many in converted Buddhist temples. Situated on small estates whose land provided revenues for their upkeep, each school had classrooms, a set of officially printed texts, and a space set aside as a temple of Confucius, where semireligious ceremonies of an edifying nature were performed. In addition, some schools possessed sizable libraries, which were open to the public: The Wuyuan County School in Liangzhe province, for example, had more than 1,400 volumes.

The local schools prepared students for the civil-service examination at the prefectural level, the first of three competitive tests designed to sift out the finest minds.

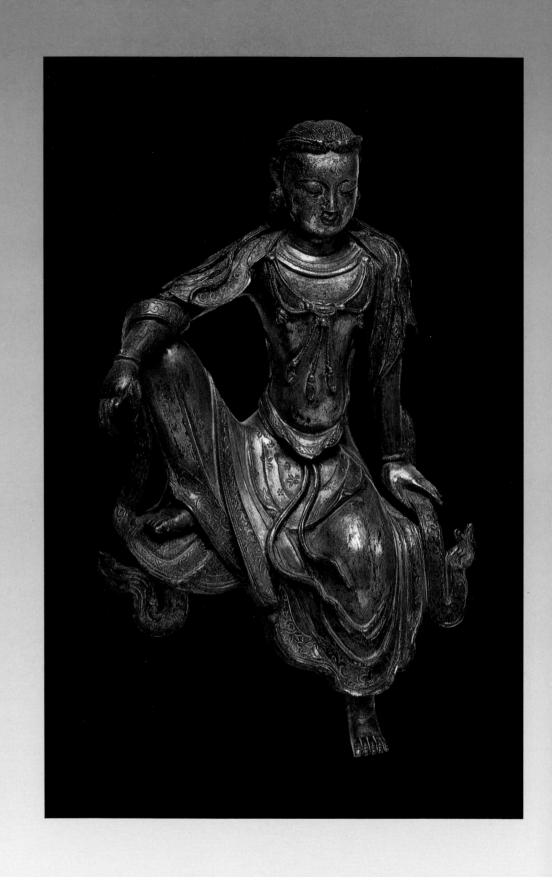

The most prestigious course of study—the one which during the century became the only route to officialdom—led to the *jinshi* examination, which involved poetry composition, essays on government policy, and elucidations of the Confucian canon. Answers to set questions on the writings of the great philosopher were learned by rote, as one surviving example shows: "Question: Confucius said of Zichan that in him were to be found four virtues that belong to the way of the gentleman. What are these virtues? Answer: In his private conduct he was courteous; in serving his master he was punctilious; in providing for the needs of the people he gave them even more than their due; in exacting service from the people he was just. I answer this question with respect."

Only a tiny minority of candidates for the prefectural examination—usually one in a hundred or fewer—could expect to go on to the next examination, which was held in Kaifeng and supervised by government officials. Here too the rate of elimination was high; fewer than 10 percent would pass. The psychological toll was correspondingly great. Before their ordeal some students prayed, but others took more direct measures to improve their chances; both cheating and favoritism were problems. Candidates were searched for crib notes before the test, and afterward clerks made copies of the papers to pass on to the examiners, thus preserving the anonymity of students with distinctive calligraphy.

The final exam was held at the imperial palace in Kaifeng in the presence of the emperor. Here the aim was to grade candidates, not to eliminate them; candidates were ranked as "passed with distinction," "formally qualified," or "passed."

Each year the government awarded about 200 palace degrees. Since the new graduates were usually in their late twenties or early thirties, the diploma crowned years of study, and the celebrations were suitably riotous. Garlanded with flowers and dressed in the green robes and new boots given to them as imperial gifts, the graduates dined and drank at many feasts, including one courtesy of the emperor himself, the Banquet in the Garden of the Beautiful Jade Grove. They composed songs and poems for these occasions. One such verse conveys the moment's drunken joy and sobering responsibility:

> The minister gave a banquet, and we indulged in happy words
>   and laughter.
> The wine bottles were empty, and our faces flushed.
> We sang like crazy, and shouted loudly at each other;
> We danced, and fell on the doorsteps.
> There was not much thinking at the time;
> All we did was to enjoy the moment.
> Soon we shall go on to the road of officialdom;
> Pray for us that we do not take our responsibility lightly.

The swirling lines of the belt and dress impart a vivid informality to this gilt bronze statue of Guanyin, goddess of mercy and compassion, which probably adorned the side of a Buddhist altar. The goddess was the Chinese incarnation of a male Indian bodhisattva, a divine being committed to the alleviation of human suffering. Although Buddhism was in relative decline during the Song era, the popularity of Guanyin—who was worshiped especially by barren women desiring children—remained undimmed.

Only a tiny elite of the nation's students—one in several thousand of the total population—attained the culminating honor of a palace degree, but those who did were virtually assured of good jobs in the civil service, while the top few students could expect in the course of their careers to attain the office of privy councilor. As such, they advised and aided the emperor, the source of all their power. Embodying the people and their government, he was in theory the font of all laws and decrees, the originator of all policy. His councilors and court stood to attention in his presence, no doubt with a certain degree of nervousness since he could promote or banish them with a word.

The focal point of Song government was the emperor's daily meeting with his Council of State, an assembly of the nation's highest-ranking officials, including the ministers of finance, justice, public works, and war. Also present were the heads of two bureaus that served respectively as the imperial voice and the imperial ear: the Chancellery and the Secretariat. The Chancellery translated policy decisions into edicts and decrees, which it issued to regional authorities, while the Secretariat processed petitions, suggestions, and complaints from across the empire for official consideration. At the meetings, the councilors deliberated and decided issues. If their debate fell into a deadlock, the emperor would make the final decision; otherwise, he simply ratified policies established by consensus.

Agreement was relatively easy to obtain in the early decades of the century, but political opinions subsequently became polarized by a power struggle that split the ranks of China's governing elite and increasingly came to dominate the nation's affairs. Its roots lay in a growing economic crisis: Revenues failed to keep pace with constantly rising government expenditure, causing a growing budget deficit.

The sources of the problem were complex and difficult to resolve. They included widespread tax evasion by the large landowners and a corresponding overtaxing of small freeholders to meet district tax quotas. Some peasants chose to give up their land and head for the cities rather than face the exactions of the taxgatherers. Meanwhile, defense spending was escalating out of control. By the mid-eleventh century, the standing army numbered well over a million men, many of them superannuated as soldiers but still drawing a regular government salary.

Debate raged over how best to redress the fiscal balance, setting reformers, who sought radical solutions in wide-ranging programs of social change, against conservatives, who defended the social and institutional status quo. The struggle between the two factions took place under the looming shadow of the Khitan and Tanguts, increasingly menacing presences as the century advanced.

It was a border crisis in 1044, when the Song bought off a threatened Tangut invasion with the offer of tribute at the same time as agreeing to increase their annual payments to the Khitan, that first brought matters to a head. The confrontation highlighted flaws in the Song defenses that in turn reflected deeper problems in the administrative system as a whole, and in its wake the reigning emperor, Renzong, turned to the reformers among his personal advisers for solutions. Their leader was Fan Zhongyan, a Confucian scholar and moralist. Fan's program included measures to improve the quality of civil-service personnel by means of performance evaluations, as well as by eliminating the patronage appointments that still played a part in the system. He also sought to improve the lot of the small freeholders and recommended the formation of local conscript militias to supplement the standing army.

Fan's motto was "The true scholar should be the first to become anxious about the world's troubles and the last to enjoy its happiness." The first concern of some of his contemporaries, however, was their own vested interest in rural estates or bureaucratic power, which was threatened by the new measures. After a few years of ascendancy, Fan and his allies were eased out of the court by antireformists.

The conflict was a mere dress rehearsal for the struggle that ensued over the policies of Wang Anshi, a noted essayist and poet who rose to power in 1069. The passage of twenty years had only aggravated the government's military and financial problems, while the entrenched bureaucracy, costly and growing, seemed ever less capable of meeting the challenge. Wang's reforms, known as the New Policies, addressed many aspects of Song society: the military, the tax system, education, trade, the money supply, and the functioning of the bureaucracy. His measures were detailed—for example, prescribing specific changes in the doctoral exams to make them more relevant to the practical needs of administrators, and organizing horse breeding to supply the cavalry. The reforms included the introduction of a graduated tax based on freshly assessed land values, low-interest state loans for peasants and small businesses, the reintroduction of village militias, and a greatly increased money supply. The program presupposed large-scale state intervention in almost every aspect of life, in Wang's view the simplest route to stimulating the economy, strengthening the military, and making the civil service more efficient.

Wang's reforms addressed most of the major problems of the time, but in so doing they ran up against the vested interests of its most influential citizens: the wealthy landowning class from whose ranks the intellectuals and administrators of Song China were principally drawn. As a result, the outcry against them was intense. Wang's opponents included not just self-interested conservatives who stood to lose financially from the changes, but also leading scholars, among them the great historian Sima Guang and the mathematician Shao Yong, who on good Confucian grounds preferred moral leadership to government interference. Wang was attacked personally for his unkempt appearance, while his policies were derided as rigid and authoritarian, concentrating power in the hands of the central government while making no accommodation for varying situations across the empire.

The New Policies were put into effect over a seven-year period during the reign of Wang's patron, Emperor Shenzong. They lasted until the ruler's death in 1086, when the empress serving as regent brought the conservatives back to power. They dismantled the previous government's work but failed to reinvigorate the old system. When Emperor Zhezong took the throne in 1093, he put Wang's policies in place once more. Although no consensus ever emerged as to whether the combined effects of Wang's policies were beneficial or harmful, it was generally agreed that the frequent changes of course imposed in the battle between the reformist and anti-reformist camps did the country little good.

The dispute over the New Policies was the greatest political storm to shake eleventh-century China, but even that conflict failed to do serious damage to the nation's highly centralized system of local administration. Via the Chancellery, the decisions of the Council of State filtered down through the governments of the 300 prefectures—administrative regions—of Song China, and thence to more than 1,200 counties. To coordinate the work of the regional authorities in the imperial scheme, the central ministries sent out circuit intendants to report on groups of prefectures. The intendants' field of investigation was limited to their specialties—fiscal, judicial, educational, commercial, or military—and the circuits overlapped so as to prevent the rise of the provincial power bases that had threatened earlier dynasties.

Like their imperial predecessors, the Song sought to ensure a high ethical standard among their civil servants and institutionalized this concern by means of official censors and remonstrators. These moral watchdogs had access to every level of the administration, including the highest. The Censorate was on guard against bribery, fraud, and other forms of corruption among officials, and had the power to impeach offenders. The Bureau of Remonstrance kept watch on the emperor himself, checking

the propriety both of his conduct and of his decrees; it had the right to censure a wayward ruler and to turn back improper edicts. The remonstrators were especially powerful in early Song times, and perhaps it is no coincidence that the period was remarkably free of the corrupting influence of the eunuchs, concubines, and favorites that were a feature of Chinese court life in other, less vigilant, eras.

The lands the Song bureaucrats administered led the world in the refinement of their civilization. As a result of the expansion of education, literacy was widespread. The technique of woodblock printing—by which the characters of a given text were carved into a reusable wooden block, then inked and stamped onto paper—had been known for centuries; now it was put to use in a wide-scale publishing industry that turned out all manner of reading material for a book-hungry public. During a fifty-year period in one small district in eastern China, for example, records show that nearly half-a-million copies of Buddhist texts and illustrations were printed. Encyclopedias, dictionaries, almanacs, and works on farming and medicine were available for the general reader, as well as books of occult healing incantations. Ambitious editions of massive religious and philosophical works—the writings of Confucius, the Daoist canon, the Buddhist Tripitaka—had been produced since the tenth century,

The painters of the Song dynasty had a vivid eye for the natural world and delighted in producing closely observed studies of plant and animal life. The painter-emperor Huizong encouraged such naturalism: A regulation issued to the court academy at the start of his reign specified that "painters should not imitate their predecessors, but should depict objects as they exist, true to form and color." In practice, realism is combined with decoration in such works as *Birds on a Thicket of Bamboo and Plum (above)*. And an affectionate sympathy enlivens beasts such as the startled hare at left, a detail of a painting by Cui Bo; and Mao Yi's cat shown guarding her kitten at right.

struck from thousands of individual woodblocks, which were used for reprinting throughout the Song dynasty. In 1005, the imperial archives possessed some 100,000 woodblocks of histories, commentaries, and sacred texts.

Sometime in the 1040s, an inventor named Bi Sheng developed a different system of printing. He fashioned individual characters in clay and baked them into pottery. He stored the countless characters in a special wooden case, arranged according to a rhyme scheme for easier retrieval. When the time came to use them, he set them in constantly varying patterns in a bed of warm, waxy resin, thereby creating the world's first movable type. However, with a language of some 40,000 separate ideographs, no system he could devise could make typesetting as efficient as the traditional method. Thus, Bi Sheng's discovery did not revolutionize printing in China as it did in Europe when Gutenberg reinvented it 400 years later. Chinese printers continued to prefer the woodblock.

The availability of texts combined with the demands of the educational system to give new life to Confucianism. In the previous centuries, this had become a somewhat academic domain, relegated largely to rote exam learning and dry exegesis, while Buddhism and Daoism had attracted a livelier following. With its elite of highly educated administrators, however, Song China needed a school of thought that addressed life in this world. Song intellectuals were drawn anew to Confucianism's secular emphasis on the moral life of man and his role in society.

Advocating both social activities and cultivation of the self, the revived doctrine was an ideal philosophy for the Song scholar-officials. In the course of the century, however, it also acquired a metaphysical dimension as a result of the labors of a small group of philosophers, who grafted onto Confucian rationalism a cosmological dimension drawn ultimately from Buddhist and Daoist beliefs. Synthesizing aspects of all three popular beliefs, the doctrine of neo-Confucianism that they founded endured for centuries as China's primary ideology.

The intellectual renaissance was paralleled by great achievements in the visual

arts. Song China's educated ruling class were avid collectors, and while some people sought out coins or ancient bronzes, others amassed paintings—watercolors in luminous hues or monochromatic studies in ink. Artists under imperial patronage largely worked in the precise, academic style favored at the court, most notably by the painter-emperor Huizong, producing highly detailed images of birds, animals, and flowers. At the same time, others preferred a larger scale, creating monumental landscapes regarded in later centuries as supreme examples of the genre. Chinese calligraphy—the writing of characters—was widely practiced as an art form, as was the related technique of depicting bamboo fronds in ink. Both required superb brushwork, whether in delicate, feathery lines or bold, vigorous strokes.

Ceramics achieved a classic perfection during the Song era. With improved firing techniques, artisans were able to supply a fast-growing market for fine porcelain as tea became a popular drink around the empire. Simplicity distinguished their creations, both in shape and color. Bowls, cups, urns, pots—all were characterized by pure, graceful silhouettes never cluttered with superfluous ornament. Sometimes restrained floral patterns were incised on their surfaces, harmonizing with their shapes. Often, though, they were left unadorned, merely glazed in white, perhaps with the faintest suggestion of blue or green.

Among the liveliest contributors to the artistic renaissance were the civil servants, who were to number among their ranks many of the century's best-known painters, essayists, poets, historians, and philosophers. An exemplar of these protean public servants was Su Shi, a civil engineer and statesman born in Sichuan in 1036.

Su Shi served the empire in many official capacities and was a leading participant in the New Policies controversy, supporting the conservative position. At the same time, using the pen name Su Dongpo, he wrote both prose and poetry that helped free contemporary literature from the rigid, stilted conventions previously in vogue. He was a master calligrapher, with a collection of over 500 kinds of ink, and he often inscribed his poems over paintings of the scenes they described, for he was also a noted landscape artist. A practitioner of both yoga and alchemy, Su Shi was interested in health and intrigued by the varying cuisines he encountered in his postings; he even wrote a cookbook. His cultivated, light-hearted voice would still echo centuries later in poems such as the one he wrote after reading the work of an earlier author:

> At first, it's just like eating tiny fish;
> What you get is hardly worth the effort.
> Then it's like the boiling of small crabs,
> Which leaves you in the end with empty claws.
> His meaning measures up to the monk Jia Dao,
> But in style he's not the equal of Han Yu.
> The life of man is brief as morning dew,
> Or a flame consuming oil day and night.
> Isn't it sad to force my two good ears
> To listen to the drone of such a miserable insect?
> I'm better off to put it all aside,
> And have some drinks of my jade-white wine.

Perhaps Song China concentrated too much on the refinements of life, at the expense of the harsh realities of military strength and defense. Certainly no Chinese emperor

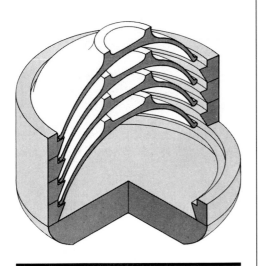

Decorated with incised lotus leaves, this twelfth-century porcelain bowl *(left)* is typical of the high-quality Ding ware produced in large quantities during the Song era. Taking its name from the modern city of Dingxian, near which the kilns were located, Ding ware is typically white with a transparent ivory glaze. After the decoration had been applied, such pieces were fired in a clay container known as a sagger, which usually held five or six bowls stacked upside down *(above).* The use of these cases increased output and also, by distributing the weight of the vessels evenly across their full diameter, reduced the tendency of the porcelain to warp as it dried out. The unglazed rims on which the bowls rested inside the sagger were finished with a band of copper or copper alloy.

THE CALLIGRAPHER'S ART

Calligraphy—the art of depicting written characters on paper—reached a high level of refinement under the Song. Drawing its inspiration from more than one art form, it was akin to literature in that many of its finest practitioners used their own poems as texts for illustration. It was even more intimately linked to painting; the same brushes and paper were used for both disciplines, and the skills demanded in forming the pictographs of the Chinese script were as much those of drawing as writing.

Working vertically downward in columns read from right to left, the artist would inscribe the characters with deft strokes on absorbent paper. A meditative mood was generally considered appropriate for the work, although the manner adopted varied from the neatly ordered to the wildly cursive. The result was a profusion of individual styles that makes the work of master calligraphers easily recognizable.

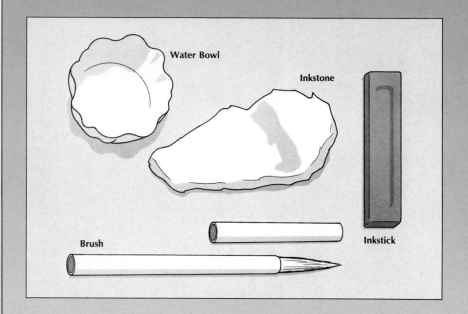

The brushes used by calligraphers were made of animal hair tied and secured in a hollow reed or bamboo stalk. Ink came in solid sticks, formed of the soot of burned pine or oil smoke mixed with gum. To apply it to paper, the artist would grind it with a little water in the hollow of an inkstone *(below, right).*

Crackle-glaze bowl for washing brushes

Polished and decorated inkstone

柳陰高士圖為
高柱浪那歡意
自豪披问伊人
何曠氏於唐居
李晉召询
丁亥夏月浩題

An eleventh-century painting by an unknown artist
portrays an inebriated
calligrapher-poet waiting
for inspiration under a wil-
low tree. A blank sheet of
paper lies in front of him,
alongside a bowl of wine.
The figure is thought to
represent a fourth-century
scholar named Tao
Yuanming, who gave up
an official post in ex-
change for the simple
pleasures of country life.

was more refined in his sensibilities or more generous in his support of the arts than the last of the Kaifeng emperors, Huizong, whose personal art collection, carefully cataloged, numbered more than 6,000 works. Yet he was to lose his throne to tough, unlettered cavalrymen and with it the northern section of the Song lands. Coming to the throne in 1101, he reigned at a time when the Jurchen tribes of eastern Manchuria were consolidating into a new empire called Jin, separated from Song China by the Khitan lands. In 1122, Huizong made a disastrous decision to ally with the new power against the old enemy. The ensuing military campaign was only too successful; the Khitan state was overwhelmed, and with it went China's buffer against the Jin.

The alliance inevitably fell apart, and within four years the Jurchen had crossed the Yellow River and laid siege to Kaifeng itself. The great capital sent out a call for relief, but the provincial armies that came to its aid were no match for the invaders. Members of the imperial household and wealthy commoners alike sent their valuables over the ramparts in an effort to buy off the enemy; the poor invaded the emperor's garden in search of food and fuel, and reports of cannibalism spread around the city. When the government finally surrendered after a six-week siege, the Jurchen agreed to withdraw in return for the payment of an enormous tribute—more, it turned out, than Song China, already drained by the war effort, could deliver. When the ransom failed to appear, the invaders stormed south once more to sack Kaifeng in 1127. By then Huizong had abdicated in favor of his son; but both the new and the old emperor were taken captive, along with 3,000 members of their court, and they subsequently died in captivity.

This disaster marked the end of the earliest and greatest period of Song history, but it did not terminate the dynasty itself. In the south, a younger son of Huizong was named emperor and eventually established his court at Hangzhou in the Yangtze delta, ceding the entire Yellow River flood plain and all the Song lands north of the Qinling Mountains to the Jurchen. Despite the loss of one third of its land area, Song culture flourished, the empire's wealth was replenished, and Hangzhou soon rivaled Kaifeng as a showcase for both. The southern Song were to prosper through the twelfth century and into the thirteenth. Then, however, a new foe, more formidable even than the Jin, was to put an end forever to Song power. In 1211, Genghis Khan would lead the Mongols in from the north, and by 1279, his grandson Kublai Khan would be the undisputed ruler of all China.

MASTERS OF INVENTION

Paper, printing techniques, gunpowder, cast iron, the magnetic compass, the paddleboat, the axial rudder, and the humble wheelbarrow were just a few of the many inventions and discoveries that were put to daily use in China centuries before they became familiar to the West. A large number of these gifts to world civilization were the fruits of the intellectual and scientific curiosity of the Song age, in the late tenth and eleventh centuries.

Breaking from the nonmaterialistic traditions of Buddhist philosophy, a major influence on Chinese thought since the fifth century, scholars of the Song period explored new fields of knowledge with a belief in the power of reason to effect progress. Cheap woodblock printing enabled their works to circulate widely through the new government schools founded to train civil servants. The imperial library alone contained over 80,000 volumes.

Many of the technological products of this intellectual endeavor were put to use in China's expanding commercial economy. Silk-reeling machines and new types of spinning wheels increased textile production. From 983, canal lock gates obviated the need to haul boats up gradients, en-abling barges to carry larger cargoes of grain and speeding their transport. A text dated 1044 describes what was possibly the world's first needle compass, a fish-shaped leaf of magnetized iron floating in a bowl of water; by the end of the century, the compass was widely used for navigation.

Another text from the same year contains the first known formula for gunpowder, which probably derived from the experiments of alchemists. And building on the ancient art of divination, which demanded a knowledge of the stars, the Chinese invented sophisticated astronomical and time-keeping instruments, of which the most spectacular was the great clock built at the imperial capital of Kaifeng in the late eleventh century.

News of these and other discoveries gradually filtered westward to Europe through trading contacts established in the course of the following centuries. Many of them—gunpowder and printing in particular—were to have revolutionary effects on Western society. Their origins, however, were often forgotten in the course of their transmission, and the wider world was slow to acknowledge its debt to the Chinese.

Iron Frame

Bamboo Wedge

Iron Plate

To print with movable type, a brush was used to mix solid ink and water in a shallow rectangular dish.

The ink was applied by brushing down the columns of characters that had been set on a type tray and wedged in place.

A sheet of paper was placed over the inked characters and rubbed down gently with a pad.

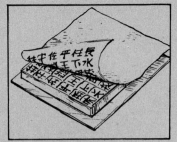

The paper was peeled away, to reveal the impression of the inked characters printed on it.

A REVOLUTION IN PRINTING

The printing technique devised by the inventor Bi Sheng in the 1040s was the world's first movable-type system. In Bi Sheng's process, individual characters, carved in clay and fired, could be rearranged to print any text required.

To keep the characters in place, Bi Sheng covered an iron plate with a sticky mixture of pine resin, wax, and paper ashes, then set a rectangular frame over it. The pieces were arranged in vertical rows inside the frame, wedged tightly together with bamboo slivers. The printer next coated them with an ink made from the soot of burned pine mixed with a gum and finally pressed paper over the form *(above)*.

The great handicap to this method, which ultimately prevented its wide use, was the vast size of the Chinese alphabet. To compose a text, the printer had to locate and arrange many thousands of individual characters. It was simpler for the Chinese to retain woodblock printing, known since the eighth century, which involved carving the entire text of a document, page by page, onto separate blocks.

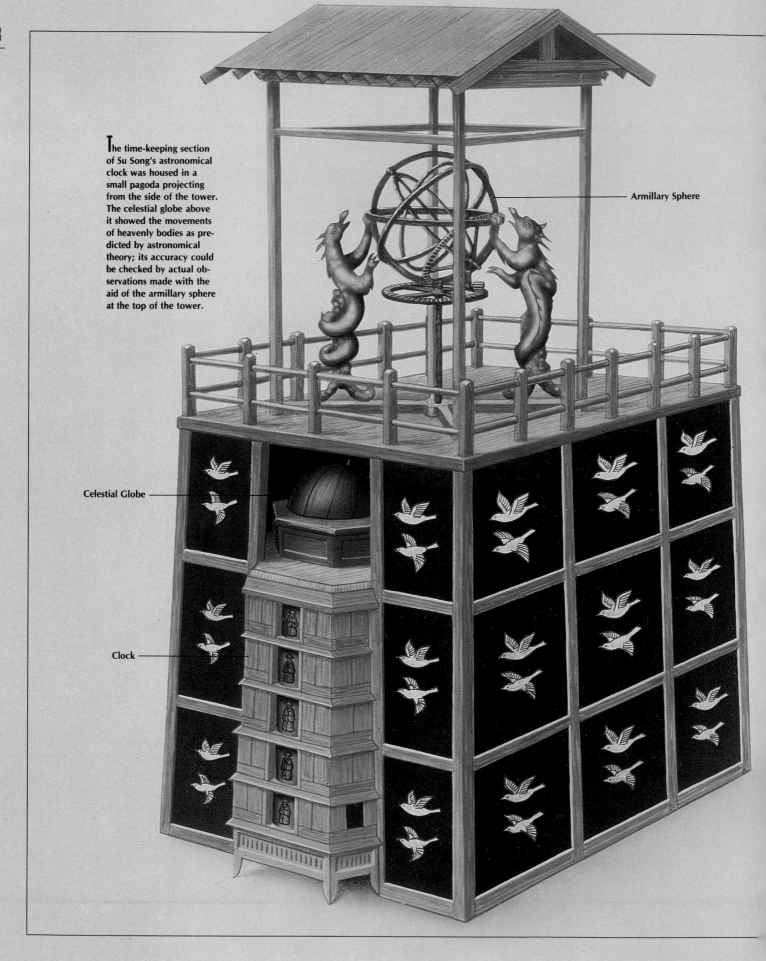

The time-keeping section of Su Song's astronomical clock was housed in a small pagoda projecting from the side of the tower. The celestial globe above it showed the movements of heavenly bodies as predicted by astronomical theory; its accuracy could be checked by actual observations made with the aid of the armillary sphere at the top of the tower.

Armillary Sphere

Celestial Globe

Clock

THE COSMIC ENGINE OF SU SONG

Shown here in cutaway, a water-powered mechanism drove the clock. Hand-cranked wheels raised the water to a series of tanks, the last kept at a constant level. From this tank a steady flow of water filled the scoops of an escapement wheel *(overleaf)*. By a gear system, this turned a vertical drive shaft that rotated the instruments.

One of the ornaments of the imperial capital of Kaifeng in the final years of the eleventh century was an extraordinary, thirty-foot-high astronomical clock, built between 1088 and 1092. The clock itself has long since disappeared, but much is known about its design and construction from the writings of its creator, an engineer named Su Song.

The clock contained three separate rotating instruments, driven by a single water-powered mechanism. One section told the time by means of puppet figures on revolving platforms who appeared with placards denoting the divisions of the hour. Another was a globe that demonstrated the movements of the heavenly bodies, which were depicted by pearls. The uppermost implement was an armillary sphere, used to observe and measure the motion of the sun, moon, and planets.

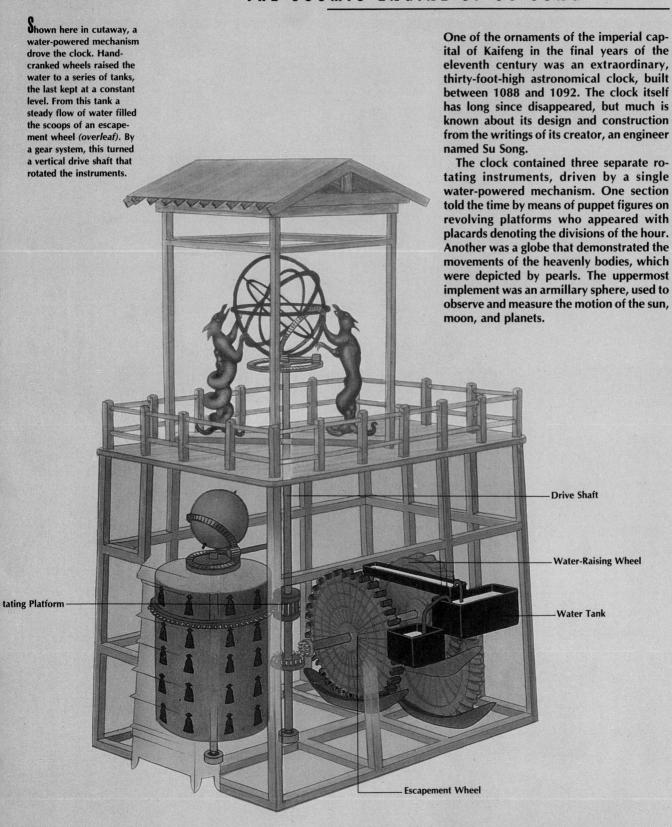

Drive Shaft

Water-Raising Wheel

Rotating Platform

Water Tank

Escapement Wheel

Reverse Brake

Gate

Counterweight

Scoop

The accuracy of Su Song's astronomical clock depended on the regular movement of the great escapement wheel. A constant-level tank fed water at uniform pressure into the thirty-six scoops on the wheel's circumference. As each scoop was filled and dropped down, it tripped a pair of levers that pulled down an upper beam and released the gate, allowing the wheel to move around for the next scoop to be filled. A reverse brake held the wheel against the gate as the scoops were filled.

Constant-Level Tank

THE ADVENT OF THE TURKS

In the late summer of 1071, news of an unprecedented disaster began to reach the rulers of Western Christendom. A Muslim force had defeated the emperor of Byzantium in a battle at Manzikert, within the Byzantine heartland of central Anatolia. The Christian forces were in disarray, and worse, the emperor himself, heir of the caesars, had been taken captive. On "that dreadful day," as contemporary chroniclers chose to call it, the empire had forfeited its historic position as the eastern bulwark of Christendom and guarantor of the pilgrimage route to Jerusalem.

Almost as startling was the fact that these Muslim invaders were not members of the Arab people, whose conquests had dismayed Europe since the seventh century. They were Seljuk Turks—nomadic horsemen who had erupted out of the steppes of central Asia barely fifty years before and subjugated present-day Iran and Iraq in little more than a single generation. Within twenty years of their triumph at Manzikert, these mounted bowmen would rule an empire that stretched from the Mediterranean to the edges of India, embracing and unifying most of the Muslim territories of Asia.

The rise of the Seljuks proved a traumatic shock for Christendom. The Turkish warriors inflicted on Byzantium a defeat from which it never fully recovered. In the wake of their victory, they were to settle Asia Minor and so to open up a corridor for the later Ottoman invasion of Europe. The threat to the eastern empire in turn galvanized the Latin West into mounting the great counteroffensive of the Crusades.

The consequences for the Muslim world were even more profound. When the Seljuks first rose to prominence, the reach of Islam was as wide as it had ever been, stretching from Spain to the Punjab and from the Caucasus Mountains to the southernmost tip of Arabia. Internally, though, the Muslim world was divided. The caliphs of Baghdad, leaders of the majority Sunni branch of the faith, had lost much of their power. By contrast, the minority Shia faction—which holds that the succession to the prophet Muhammad passed not to the caliphs, but to an alternative line of imams descended from Ali, Muhammad's son-in-law—was temporarily in the ascendant. Its supporters included the Fatimids, powerful rulers of Egypt, who had set up their own rival caliphate in Cairo. Even Baghdad itself had fallen in 946 to the Shiite Buyid dynasty, although they consented to rule in the Sunni caliph's name.

As champions of Sunni Islam, the Seljuks were to reinvigorate the sickly Baghdad caliphate and to deal a severe blow to the Shiite cause. The Seljuks' pious determination to eradicate the influence of Shiism saw them establish an educational system that nurtured some of the finest thinkers of the age. Unpracticed in the arts of government themselves, they introduced a new kind of state based on a partnership between warriors and bureaucrats—the latter mostly Persians, who spread their language and culture throughout the empire.

The Seljuks were not the first Turks to make their mark on world events. In the sixth

In one of the earliest examples of Islamic book illustration, the constellation Sagittarius is represented as a centaur drawing a double-curved bow of the type used by the Seljuk Turks—Islamic warriors who irrupted into Persia from their central Asian home to create an eleventh-century empire. Such astronomical charts drew on both classical Greek texts and the practical knowledge of the heavens gleaned by generations of Bedouins, who believed that the stars had been assigned by Allah to help them navigate the desert by night.

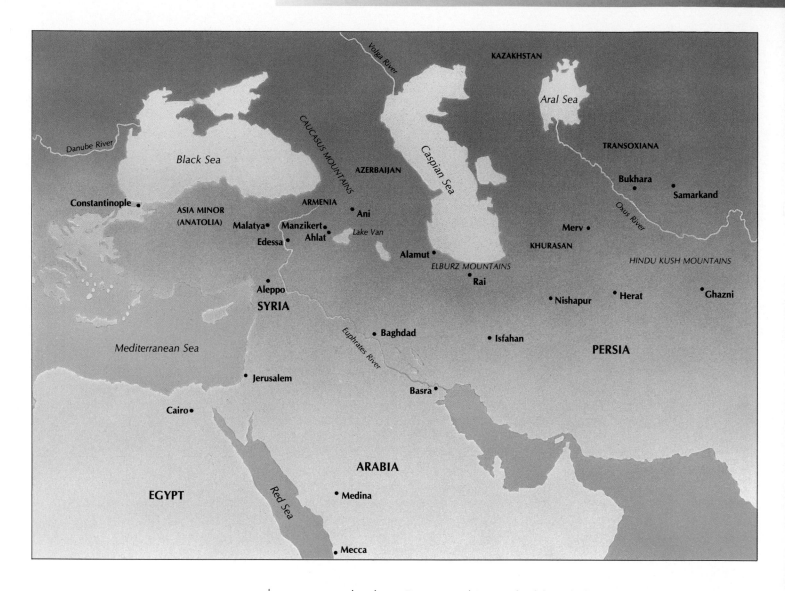

century, two brothers, Bumen and Istami, had founded a realm, later to be known as the Old Turkish Empire, centered in the steppe region of central Asia. Although at its apogee the empire stretched from the northern frontier of China to the shores of the Black Sea, it was never in fact more than a confederation of autonomous tribes, possessing no common capital, recognizing no formal boundaries, and obeying no law other than the orders of temporary military leaders called khans.

One of these tribes was named the Oghuz, and from them the Seljuks were to trace their descent. Based originally in Mongolia, the Oghuz moved westward during the eighth century, making their way to the Siberian steppes north of the Caspian and Aral seas, in present-day Soviet Kazakhstan. In later years, the Oghuz past was glorified in *The Book of Dede Korkut,* a collection of tales portraying a heroic race living in gold-decorated tents and possessing falcons, rich robes, and jewelry, and armies of slaves of both sexes.

The reality was less romantic. Like all the Turkic tribes, the Oghuz were nomadic herders. Their economy was based on sheep and the two-humped Bactrian camels, which were driven long distances to and from the summer and winter pastures. Much of their life was spent on their hardy little horses, on which they herded their livestock, fought, ate, held meetings, and even slept. They had scant knowledge of iron at this period, tipping their arrows with sharpened bone; nonetheless, the missiles could kill from prodigious distances when fired from their short bows, whose tips curved away from the archer for extra drawing power. Urban existence was alien to them. They were fascinated by towns, much as the wolf in winter is drawn to the animal pen: Towns were something to break into, plunder, and then escape from. The wolf, in fact, was one of their many totems.

In their religious beliefs, these steppe predators were animist. The Oghuz conceived of the world as divided into realms of hostile and benign forces that could be manipulated by tribal shamans, who by means of trances could exorcise the evil spirits dwelling below the earth and win the protection of the benign powers living above it. At the same time, they acknowledged the existence of a sky god called Tengri and believed in a kind of afterlife.

Ahmad ibn Fadlan, an emissary of the caliph of Baghdad who journeyed through Oghuz territory at the beginning of the tenth century, described the funeral rites that followed the death of one of their leaders. After the dead man had been entombed, in company with his possessions and a wooden drinking cup of intoxicating liquor, up to 200 horses would be slaughtered and eaten; the heads, hoofs, hides, and tails would then be hung above the tomb on wooden poles, alongside carved wooden effigies of all the enemies the deceased warrior had slain. "These are his steeds on which he rides to paradise," the mourners would shout. "These are his pages who serve him in paradise."

In other respects, the lifestyle Ibn Fadlan described was less impressive. According to him, the Oghuz lived in tents of plain felt (probably similar to the yurts used by present-day Mongolian nomads) and customarily wore their clothes until they disintegrated from age. Their sick either were left to recover as best they could or were turned out to die. They never washed; indeed, the Arab noted, they had nothing whatever to do with water, especially in the wintertime. They had a strict code of moral behavior, and sexual misconduct was dealt with swiftly and severely: If an adulterer was discovered, the Oghuz would tie the offender to bent tree branches, then release them to tear him in two.

Ibn Fadlan was by no means the first Arab to encounter the Oghuz. The Islamic world had long been familiar with them and other Turkic peoples as caravan guides, steppe traders, and soldiers. They were particularly prized for their formidable fighting qualities, and it was in the guise of mercenaries in Islam's armies that they entered the fold of civilization.

When Ibn Fadlan first encountered the nomadic Oghuz, they were living near the Volga River, which served as a boundary between their domain and the land of the Khazars, a Turkic people whose aristocracy had been won over to a kind of Judaism. Probably the Oghuz became vassals or mercenaries of the Khazars: The first known reference to Seljuk, the founder of the dynasty that was to bear his name, dates from the tenth century and describes him as the offspring of a warrior in the service of the Khazars. "There was a son born to this man," records the *Malik-nama*, a semi-legendary history of the family commissioned later by the victor of Manzikert, "and

he called him Seljuk, and he was brought up in the palace, and he loved him greatly."

Much of the early history of the Seljuks is unclear, but it seems that, following a rift with the Khazars or with other Oghuz, they moved to the borders of Iran. There a momentous change took place. In the words of one chronicle, the tribes "went forth from the land of Turan, that is to say of the Turks, to the land of Iran, that is to say of the Persians, under the pretense that they were shepherds. And when they saw that Persia was flourishing with Islam, they took counsel together and said: 'If we do not enter the Faith of the people in the country in which we desire to live and make a pact with them, no man will cleave to us, and we shall be a small and solitary people.' " Thus, sometime in the late tenth century, Seljuk's clan became converted to Islam, to be followed by the other Oghuz clans.

The depth of their initial conversion is questionable; Seljuk himself is said still to have turned to a shaman to interpret his dreams. It may even have been his second change of faith to a religion of the Bible; three of his sons—Mikhail (Michael), Israil, and Musa (Moses)—bore names that reflect either a Khazar Jewish influence or the teachings of Nestorian Christian missionaries from Persia. Nonetheless, there were to be no further shifts of religious allegiance, and the zeal with which the Seljuk family embraced the Sunni branch of Islam was in the long run to prove as momentous for the future of the Middle East as the conversion of Clovis and his Franks was to Christian Europe.

The region into which Seljuk led his followers was called Transoxiana, or the "Land beyond the Oxus River." It was a border region where the Islamic world had traditionally confronted the territories of the nomadic Turks—"two elements, fire and water, which rage against each other in the depths of the heart," according to Firdausi, Persia's great eleventh-century poet. The Islamic states had taken special pains to secure this frontier, and for three centuries, Transoxiana had flourished, its major cities of Samarkand and Bukhara rising to fame and wealth under the rule of the Samanids, a Muslim dynasty of Persian origin. By the time of the Seljuks' conversion, however, the Samanid dynasty was in decline, a spent power dependent for its defense on Turkomans—a term used at the time to distinguish Muslim Turkish auxiliaries from their pagan counterparts. The Seljuks were one such group; before long, they were vying with the others for position in a land that provided ample scope for military opportunists.

Their most fearsome rivals among the other Islamized Turks were the followers of a breakaway dynasty set up in the southern city of Ghazni, in present-day Afghanistan. These Ghaznavids produced a mighty leader in Mahmud of Ghazni, one of the dominant personalities of the early eleventh century. Throughout Seljuk's lifetime, the power of the Ghaznavids dwarfed that of his own people, who remained little more than a warrior band, though one growing in size and strength. After his death at the reputed age of 107, his heirs made the error of offering their services to a rival Turkic group, which was vanquished by Mahmud in 1025.

Chroniclers record that at some point—possibly in the wake of that defeat—Mahmud met with Seljuk's son and heir, who bore the name of Arslan ("Lion"), and asked him how many men he could muster to his service. In reply, the Seljuk leader produced two arrows from his quiver and boasted that he could summon 100,000 men to arms if he sent the missiles among his people and double that number if he sent his bow. Alarmed, Mahmud turned for advice to one of his counselors, who

Unencumbered by body armor and carrying only a light wooden shield for defense, a Seljuk irregular cavalryman used his superior mobility to outmaneuver enemy foot soldiers and troopers. Taught to ride in earliest childhood, he developed an extraordinary empathy with his small, wiry pony, which would halt, turn, or change direction instantly upon command. The cavalryman's silk wrap-over topcoat, worn over felt breeches and divided below the waist, was designed for comfort on horseback. His fur-trimmed silk cap provided warmth. His main weapon was a short, double-curved bow, but for hand-to-hand combat, he also carried a double-edged sword and an iron-headed mace.

suggested that each man's thumbs should be amputated so that he could no longer draw a bow. Mahmud, whose most celebrated exploit was the storming, amid frightful carnage, of one of India's wealthiest Shiva temples, was entirely capable of issuing the command for such a brutal act; but even he found the proposal impracticable. Instead, he sought to monitor the growing strength of the clan by bringing the Seljuks within his own orbit of power. In order to achieve that end, he allowed Arslan, accompanied by 4,000 families and all their baggage and animals, to cross the Oxus River into the Persian region of Khurasan.

Mahmud had miscalculated badly. From their base in Khurasan, the Seljuks were soon plundering settled lands all over northern Persia. In an attempt to restrain them, Mahmud took as hostage Arslan, who died in a Ghaznavid fortress on the borders of India. The Seljuk depredations continued, however: The clan ruined agriculture with their flocks, held towns for ransom, and—in the words of a twelfth-century Persian historian—"devoured Khurasan as if it were food laid out for hunting falcons." In 1029, Mahmud mounted a campaign to drive them back across the Oxus, but although he defeated them on the field of battle, most of the Seljuks managed to elude him and scattered across Persia.

Mahmud died the following year. By that time, the Seljuks were divided; one group had traveled to Azerbaijan, where they supported themselves as mercenary soldiers in the employment of local princes. Another body, under the leadership of two nephews of Arslan called Chaghri-Beg and Tughril-Beg, had retreated to the steppeland south of the Aral Sea. From there, they petitioned Mahmud's heir, Masud—of whom it was said that he inherited only his father's vices—to be allowed to return to Khurasan. When permission was refused, they took matters into their own hands and returned in force, crossing the Oxus in 1035 with 10,000 horsemen. With them were

The Mounted Archer's Deadly Skills

In their skill with the bow and their reliance on it as their principal weapon, the Seljuks conducted battle in a central Asian tradition that had originated more than 1,000 years earlier. One of their favorite tactics, the retreat covered by the so-called Parthian shot over the horse's tail, had been used by mounted archers against the armies of Alexander the Great. This and other standard maneuvers, some of which are illustrated here, were practiced from childhood onward by the Turks.

By any standard, the Seljuk archers' accuracy and rate of fire were remarkable—all the more so because they often loosed their arrows while riding at full gallop, even hanging under their horses' necks to avoid enemy fire. A crusader who encountered them in battle observed that they "shoot faster than could be believed," and an Arab traveler who witnessed their marksmanship reported that he had seen one of their commanders string a bow while in the saddle and then shoot dead a goose flying overhead.

In long-range fighting, the Seljuks were all but invincible. Their only enemy was rain, for a dampened bowstring became slack and useless.

Forward slanted shot

many foot soldiers from other Oghuz tribes who had pledged their support to the new chiefs. Once in Khurasan, the Seljuk forces ravaged the land exactly as they had done before. "No district . . . is able to support them for more than a week because of their vast number," wrote a Christian chronicler, "and from sheer necessity they are compelled to depart to another quarter to find food for themselves and their beasts." In Chaghri-Beg and Tughril-Beg, however, the Seljuks had found leaders who were no longer content to plunder and then move on to fresh pastures; they wanted nothing less than territorial sovereignty.

To get it, they resorted to terrorizing the native population into submission, while at the same time setting themselves up as champions of Sunni Islam. The dual strategy of wielding the sword and the Book worked. Already impoverished by the exactions of the Ghaznavids, local leaders threw themselves on the mercy of these new invaders, hoping that the Seljuks would then turn their attention to other targets. In this way, Nishapur, the capital of Khurasan, and the ancient trading city of Merv both fell to the Seljuks in 1037.

Masud perceived too late the threat to his territories. He sent troops against the Seljuks, but they were too slow-moving to catch the horsemen in the desert terrain. The Turks pursued a deliberate policy of evasion, summed up by a later Persian historian who put these words in the mouths of their leaders: "It is unwise to seek a pitched battle with this sovereign. Let us keep to our own way and not be burdened with baggage and impediments. In this way we will gain the preponderance. We will not disperse, unless some difficulty arises, so let him go backward, just as he wishes. Winter has passed and summer has begun; we are steppe dwellers and are well able to endure extremes of heat and cold, whereas he and his army cannot, and after suffering this distress for a while, will have to turn back."

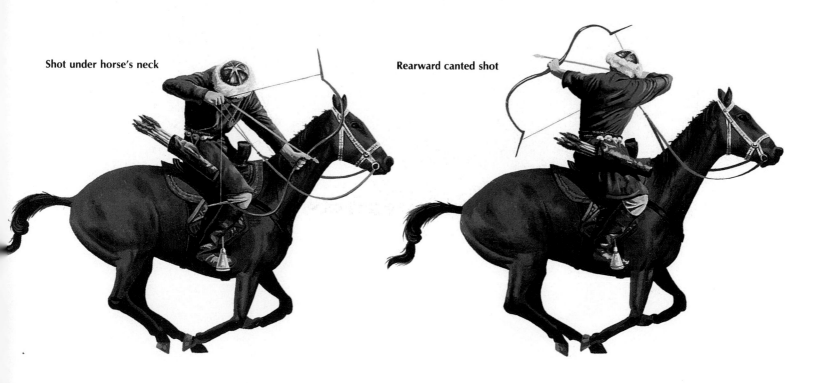

Shot under horse's neck

Rearward canted shot

By 1040, the Seljuks' strategy of evasion had proved so successful in wearing down the Ghaznavid armies that they felt strong enough to risk engaging in a full-scale battle. On the plain of Dandanqan, north of Merv, they routed the Ghaznavids. Masud fled to India where, his spirit broken, he lived out the days remaining to him sunk in wine and music.

Now not just Khurasan but the whole of the Iranian plateau lay open to the Seljuks. Their leaders chose to divide and conquer. Chaghri-Beg kept Khurasan itself and enlarged his territories by reoccupying the land south of the Aral Sea, while at the same time keeping the Ghaznavids and other Turkoman forces at bay. Tughril-Beg turned his attention to the west. Aided by Ibrahim Inal, a kinsman, he seized Rai (a suburb of present-day Tehran) and established suzerainty over Isfahan between 1040 and 1044. He now had the choice of pursuing either one of the important trade routes leading westward across the Iranian plateau—one headed toward Baghdad, the other in the direction of Azerbaijan, Armenia, and Byzantine Asia Minor. Realizing that he could win over his new Persian subjects only by restricting the pillaging of his soldiery, he settled on the northern route and spent most of the next ten years directing his operations against the Christians of Armenia, a mountainous land recently annexed into the Byzantine Empire.

Tughril-Beg's ultimate objective, however, was the city of Baghdad itself. The seat of the Abbasid caliphs was now in practice under the control of Basasiri, a general in the service of the Shiite Buyids. Determined to restore the caliph's independence and win power and glory for himself, Tughril-Beg marched on the capital in 1055. The city soon capitulated, and Basasiri and his troops took flight. Tughril immediately assumed the Buyids' temporal powers while offering devout obeisance to the caliph as the leader of Islam. In return, the caliph conferred on Tughril-Beg the title of sultan.

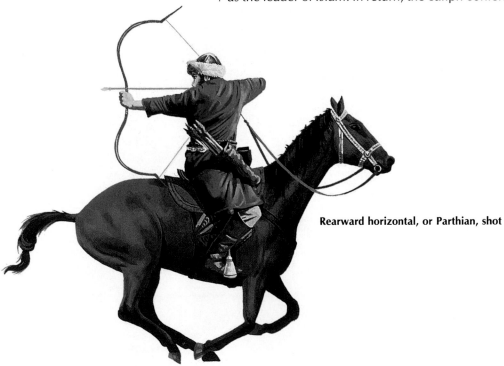

Rearward horizontal, or Parthian, shot

To seal the relationship, the caliph took one of the sultan's nieces to be his wife.

Trouble soon flared, however, when Tughril-Beg had to leave the city to quell an Oghuz revolt. Provoked by the excesses of the undisciplined Turkish rank and file, the population of Baghdad took advantage of the sultan's absence to transfer their loyalty back to Basasiri. It was only a temporary reverse for Tughril-Beg, who in 1059, after putting down the rebellion, fought his way back into Baghdad, killed Basasiri, and restored the Abbasid caliph to the throne. In reward, he demanded one of the caliph's daughters in marriage, but on the eve of the ceremony in 1063, at the age of about seventy, he died of a hemorrhage, leaving no children.

Several rival claimants sought to fill the ensuing power vacuum. The victor was Tughril's nephew Alp Arslan ("Heroic Lion"), who had already inherited the eastern Seljuk realm upon the death of his father, Chaghri-Beg; so the Seljuk forces were once more united under a single leader. The rivals, who had included his cousin Kutul-mush and his father's vizier, or chief minister, were duly dispatched; Kutulmush died in unknown circumstances, while the vizier was executed. Alp Arslan replaced him with a minister of his own choosing. The new vizier was known simply by his title, Nizam al-Mulk, "the Order of the Kingdom," and that is precisely what this wise and powerful administrator guaranteed for the next twenty years.

At the time of his succession in 1063, Alp Arslan was about thirty-three. He was a commanding figure, with mustaches so long that he had to tie them behind his tall Persian cap to prevent them from interfering with his archery. By his Muslim flatterers he was considered warlike, provident, firm, just, and distinguished by other excellent qualities; his Christian detractors characterized him as a "drinker of blood" and a warrior of the Antichrist. A revealing insight into Alp Arlsan's character was provided by Nizam al-Mulk when the vizier asked his sultan why he did not appoint an informer to spy on factions within the court. "If I appoint an informer," the sultan replied, "those who are my sincere friends and enjoy my intimacy will not pay any attention to him nor bribe him, trusting in their fidelity, friendship, and intimacy. On the other hand, my adversaries and enemies will make friends with him and give him money: It is clear that the informer will be constantly bringing me bad reports of my friends and good reports of my enemies. Good and bad words are like arrows; if several are shot, at least one hits the target; every day, my sympathy with my friends will diminish and that to my enemies increase. Within a short time, my enemies will be nearer to me than my friends and will finally take their place."

Alp Arslan was certainly surrounded by potential enemies and faced with imme-diate problems. He ruled a land that covered almost all of present-day Iran and Iraq, territories that included in Baghdad and the Persian cities some of the wealthiest and most civilized centers of the eleventh-century world. The economic strength of his empire depended on Arab and Persian cultivators and merchants, so it was essential that he maintain peace and order within his frontiers. On the other hand, Alp Arslan's military strength still rested with the steppe-born nomads for whom pillaging was a way of life and who gave him their allegiance only in return for the prospect of booty. To make matters worse, the original Seljuk army, which responded to at least a modicum of discipline, had been followed across the Oxus by swarms of other Turkomans who fought his Arab and Persian subjects for possession of wells and grazing lands and plundered the caravans that helped swell his imperial coffers.

Like his uncle Tughril-Beg, Alp Arslan sought external enemies to divert Turkoman violence away from his own dominion. There were three main targets for him to

MANZIKERT, AUGUST 1071

Alp Arslan

SELJUKS

Romanus

BYZANTINES

The battle that opened up Asia Minor to the Seljuks was a triumph of mobility over fixed-formation fighting. Shown here in its climactic final stage, the engagement had started several hours earlier and seven and a half miles away, when the Byzantine emperor Romanus led his 40,000-strong army out of Manzikert, which is the modern-day village of Malazgirt, in the arid wastelands of eastern Turkey.

In battle-proved Byzantine tradition, Romanus had disposed his forces in two compact lines, marching several hundred yards apart. He himself commanded the vanguard, giving charge of the rear guard to his bitter political rival Andronicus. The battle order was basically defensive, designed to absorb the shock of an enemy charge by allowing the vanguard to fall back without disorder into spaces left between the rearguard troops.

The Seljuks, however, who were drawn up in a loose crescent formation, declined to press home a general attack. Instead, they harried the Byzantines with swarms of arrows, withdrawing when threatened, luring the enemy ever closer to an upland ridge where the Seljuk sultan Alp Arslan watched and waited.

As the evening shadows lengthened, Romanus realized that further pursuit would be futile and signaled a general retreat by reversing the imperial standard. Some of the men on the wings took the signal to mean that he had fallen, and they broke ranks, spreading panic.

At the same moment, Alp Arslan launched an attack with his reserves, who had been kept hidden in the broken terrain below his command post. They cut their way between the center and the right wing, isolating the front line from the rear guard, which promptly turned and fled (diagram, inset), encouraged by the treacherous Andronicus. By nightfall, most of the Byzantine vanguard had been put to the sword, and the emperor himself was a prisoner of the Seljuks.

attack: his uncle's chosen target of Armenia; Byzantine Asia Minor, with a central plateau ideally suited to nomadic pastoralism; and Fatimid Egypt, the home of the Shiite anticaliphate. At first, Alp Arslan chose to imitate his uncle; he led his first major campaign as sultan against Armenia, occupying the old capital of Ani in 1064. For the rest of the decade, he contented himself with desultory warfare against the Byzantines of Asia Minor, limiting his operations to the frontier zone and the recovery of border strongholds.

The sultan apparently had no intention of conquering Asia Minor as a whole. To him, as to the other Islamic leaders of the Middle East, it was Christian territory—or, as they called it, Rum, ("Rome") in enduring memory of the old Roman Empire. Its religious affiliation did not automatically make it a target for conquest. The Koran enjoins Muslims to respect members of the other monotheistic religions, and in the mid-eleventh century, this injunction was generally observed. Unlike the Byzantine Empire itself, which attempted to enforce religious uniformity on all its citizens, most Muslim states of the period were prepared to tolerate religious minorities provided they were "People of the Book," in other words Jews, Zoroastrians, or Christians.

Alp Arslan was much less tolerant of schismatics within his own faith. His strongest ambition was to wage jihad, or holy war, on the Shiite schismatics of Egypt. With this goal in mind, he apparently negotiated a truce with Byzantium, for in late 1070 or early 1071, confident that his empire was not threatened, he led an army southward. By March, he was besieging Edessa in what would later be southeastern Turkey. A Byzantine emissary visited his camp there with further reassurances of the Byzantine emperor's peaceful intentions. Convinced, the sultan continued toward Egypt, completely unaware that even as he and the emissary were discussing terms, the emperor had left Constantinople at the head of a large army and was marching across Asia Minor to recover the Armenian strongholds and border forts he had lost to the Seljuks.

If art and commerce are the mirrors of civilization, then Byzantium in the middle of the eleventh century stood at the pinnacle of her greatness. With the possible exception of China and the Islamic lands themselves, there was no power on earth so well administered or so wealthy. From Italy and Egypt, Russia and Germany, merchants came to Constantinople to exchange their own crude goods for the enamels, silks, and purples produced in the capital's factories. They never failed to be awed by the sophistication of its inhabitants, the comfort of its suburban houses, the magnificence of its churches and palaces. To them the city of Constantinople seemed to be the center of the universe.

The splendor of Byzantium, however, rested on shaky foundations. After the death in 1025 of the warrior-emperor Basil II, who had pushed back the boundaries of the empire to the Danube River in the north, southern Italy in the west, and Armenia in the east, the throne had passed to a succession of weaker rulers who were unwilling or unable to defend his hard-won frontiers. The military machine Basil had built up was starved of funds by a civilian administration that feared it, while the nobility's greed for estates accomplished the destruction of the themes—provinces occupied by yeomen peasant-soldiers whose vested interest in the land had made them the backbone of the nation's defense. At the time that Alp Arslan became sultan, the Byzantine throne was occupied by Constantine X Ducas, a puppet of the civil administration who had reduced the regular armed forces until the empire was almost totally reliant for its defense on foreign mercenaries. Upon the death of Constantine in 1067, even

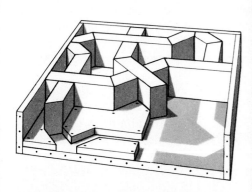

Under the Seljuks, Islamic artists evolved new techniques for creating intricately patterned brickwork, such as this facade of an eleventh-century tomb in western Iran. The most complex designs were made in sections by specialists and set into place after the main structure had been built. First, the bricks were arranged face down in a wooden frame *(above)*; to create dramatic relief effects, wooden blocks were placed beneath and between some of them. Gypsum plaster was then laid over them to cast them into a panel; once the plaster had hardened, the wooden frame was removed. Square holes for scaffolding were left in the structural walls, making it easier for the builders to fix the finished panels into place.

the civilian authorities had recognized the danger and compelled his widow, Eudocia, to marry a man who would be capable of restoring the imperial defenses. She chose the son of a distinguished military family, Romanus Diogenes—a brave and handsome soldier, whose "very breath seemed noble, if not actually divine," according to one of his admirers.

Three years of inglorious and mainly ineffectual campaigning on the eastern frontier against the Seljuks and other independent Turkoman raiders demonstrated how low the army's fighting capability had fallen. Nevertheless, when news of the Seljuk move on Egypt reached Romanus, he could not resist the opportunity to regain his Armenian territories, and he lost no time in assembling the largest military force he had yet taken into the field.

With the conscript army of the themes largely a thing of the past, Byzantine military power was based on a heterogeneous collection of units, several of which had fought against one another in the past. Impressive on paper, with a strength estimated at between 60,000 and 100,000 men, Romanus's host was in fact a collection of ill-disciplined units. The native troops of the imperial guard—the standing army kept on permanent duty in the environs of Constantinople—made up about half the force. But, after years of neglect, these professional soldiers were badly disciplined and poorly armed; and their chief captain was the former emperor's nephew Andronicus Ducas, a bitter enemy of Romanus, who took him along only because he thought it would be unsafe to leave him plotting in Constantinople. The rest of Romanus's force consisted of mercenaries, of which the greatest number were non-Seljuk Turks. The other contingents included a Norman heavy cavalry squadron under the command of a renowned mercenary captain, Roussel of Bailleul, as well as Norsemen, Armenians, Bulgars, and Germans.

Dissension soon broke out among the different groups, and morale plummeted as they marched through regions devastated by Seljuk raiders the year before. Romanus did his best to maintain order, but the strain told on him during the weary, three-month march across Asia Minor. According to Attaleiates, a veteran of the campaign who subsequently wrote an account of it, the emperor made "a stranger of himself to his own army," setting up his own camp apart from the rest of the troops.

Alp Arslan learned of the emperor's advance early in the month of May, when he had reached the Syrian town of Aleppo. He immediately abandoned his campaign against Egypt and hurried back to the north with only his personal guard of some 4,000 men, recrossing the Euphrates in such haste that most of his horses and pack animals were lost in the process.

Romanus was nearing the eastern frontier with Armenia when he received word of Alp Arslan's turnabout. Confident that he could capture and garrison the border strongholds before the sultan could raise reinforcements, he made the fateful decision to advance beyond Byzantine territory in an attempt to regain the border fortresses lost in recent years to the Turks.

On reaching the frontier zone, Romanus divided his forces. The Frankish cavalry under Roussel was dispatched to capture Ahlat, on the northern shore of Lake Van, from its Turkish defenders. He himself led the rest of the army to Manzikert, almost thirty miles to the north. The present-day village of Malazgirt in eastern Turkey, Manzikert was a key stronghold commanding the main route into Asia Minor from the east. Anticipating an easy victory there, Romanus sent almost all his infantry to reinforce Roussel. It seemed a reasonable decision, for Manzikert itself fell without a fight. After allowing the inhabitants of the city to evacuate it unharmed, the emperor garrisoned the fort and returned to his camp to receive the acclamations of his troops. He went to sleep that night not knowing how things had fared at Ahlat, but reassured by the conviction that his chief adversary, Alp Arslan, must still be far away.

In fact, the Seljuk troops were within a day's ride of Manzikert. Alp Arslan had sent his vizier, Nizam al-Mulk, to muster reinforcements, while he himself had traveled by an unknown route to Lake Van, picking up additional troops en route. He seems to have reached the vicinity of Ahlat as Roussel's Franks approached it. There may or may not have been an engagement between the two forces; what is certain is that the Frankish cavalry and the infantry reinforcements both took to their heels, hardly pausing until they reached Malatya, more than ninety miles to the west. They apparently made no attempt either to rejoin the emperor or even to send couriers with news of their withdrawal.

Romanus did not learn of the Seljuk presence until the day after he had taken Manzikert, when one of his foraging parties came under attack. Assuming that it had run into an isolated unit of Turkish raiders, he sent only a small force, under the command of one of his generals, Bryennius, to drive off the enemy. Word soon came back that the Turks were more numerous than had been expected, whereupon the emperor ordered an Armenian officer, Basilacius, to lead a reconnaissance in force. Recklessly, Basilacius attempted to engage the enemy, losing touch with Bryennius in the process. The Turks fell back, but only so as to lead the Byzantines into an ambush. Basilacius fell into the trap; he was taken prisoner, and his detachment was slaughtered almost to a man. Attempting a rescue, Bryennius came under fierce attack himself and barely escaped with his life, returning to camp with a lance wound in his chest and two arrows in his back armor. At last, Romanus knew that he was up against Alp Arslan's entire army.

That night, the Seljuks attacked some of the emperor's Turkish mercenaries who had strayed beyond the fortifications of the emperor's camp outside Manzikert, forcing them to flee back inside. Panic spread among the other soldiers, who thought the base itself was being assaulted. "It was then," records Attaleiates, "that a tremendous fear took over; there was talk of disaster, there were incoherent cries, meaningless shouting; it was a scene of utter confusion and impending doom." The following day, a contingent of Turks went over to the sultan's army, arousing fears that all the Turks would defect.

This bronze ewer in the form of a gaping lion was used to pour water for the ritual washing of hands before prayer enjoined upon Muslims by the Koran. Known as aquamaniles, the jugs greatly impressed the Crusaders, who created a fashion for similar animal-shaped vessels in western Europe in the twelfth century.

At this critical juncture, a delegation—sent, no doubt, at Alp Arslan's instigation—arrived quite unexpectedly at Romanus's camp; claiming to speak in the name of the caliph of Baghdad, the emissaries proposed a truce. But the emperor was still expecting that Roussel's elite cavalry and the greater part of the Byzantine infantry would come to his aid. He knew how the hostile court at Constantinople would react if he returned home with nothing but a questionable treaty to show for all his efforts and expense. Furthermore, the offer suggested that Alp Arslan, who could not have had more than 40,000 men under his command, was doubtful about his own chances of achieving a victory. Confident that he could defeat the sultan's forces in a pitched battle, Romanus rebuffed the delegation's peace proposal.

Each side was familiar with the tactics that the other would employ. Byzantine rules for engaging light cavalry had been laid down in the *Tac-*

Readings from the Heavens

One of the principal achievements of medieval Muslim scientists was the development of astronomical instruments for use in everyday life. Simple celestial watches in the form of handy quadrants *(right and below)* and sundials *(opposite, below)* were used to tell time, while the more sophisticated astrolabe *(opposite, above)* could also measure the movement of planets—essential for the calculation of horoscopes by which many Muslims ordered their lives.

Borrowed from the Greeks, the astrolabe had become quite complex in form by the eleventh century. Around the rim of the face were marked the degrees of the circle. An inner rotatable disk had a beautifully designed star map and a pointer for sighting on the sun or other heavenly bodies. A ring at the top served to suspend the instrument while the measurement of angular elevation was being made. To help interpret the observation for astrological purposes, the back of the astrolabe was engraved with a zodiacal table delineating symbols for the seven planets known to medieval Arab astronomers.

Sighted on the sun, this quadrant was used to tell the time. A bead on the plumb line was adjusted against the zodiacal markings on the intrument's leading edge. The line then hung freely, and the time was shown by the position of the bead against the hour lines engraved on the quandrant's face.

A small brass quadrant was used mainly as a simple clock. Equipped with a degree scale, sights, and a plumb line *(not shown)*, it could measure the angular elevation of the sun.

This Persian-made astrolabe was used mainly to study the movement of the planets, essential for drawing up horoscopes. Beautifully designed, the instruments were referred to as "mathematical jewels."

This portable sundial was calibrated for use at the latitude of Aleppo in Syria. Such devices were used by sultan and servant alike to determine the hours of the five daily prayers.

tica of Leo the Wise as early as the ninth century. The Byzantine forces should keep together in a single body several ranks deep. To take advantage of the Byzantine's heavier armor and superior skills in hand-to-hand combat, the enemy should be engaged at close quarters as soon as possible. Cover against enemy archers should be provided by light infantry armed with heavy bows. Close communications should be maintained at all times, and the flanks should be protected if at all possible by natural defenses.

These precepts suggest how much the Byzantines feared the greater mobility of troops such as the Turks, who always tried to commit the foe to an unfavorable position while retaining their own freedom to break off or engage as circumstances dictated. Armored lightly, if at all, and mounted on their small, superbly trained horses, which could easily travel forty miles in a day, the Turks' main tactic was to ride rings around an enemy army, harrying it from a distance with swarms of arrows. Against heavily armored troops, these attacks seldom inflicted many casualties, but the constant rain of missiles imposed a nervous strain that frequently provoked a panicky retreat or stung the enemy into a reckless assault. If they were charged by a superior force, the Turks simply retreated, firing over their horses' tails as they rode, then regrouped at a safe distance and resumed their harrying tactics, like flies that could be beaten off but not destroyed. One of their most effective tactics was a feigned retreat of the type employed against Basilacius, a maneuver designed to weary a pursuing force or draw it into a trap. Such retreats might last five minutes or as many days. Only when the Turks were certain that they had gained every possible advantage over their opponents did they commit themselves to close combat with lance, sword, and club.

Shortly after noon—a Friday, August 19 or 26, 1071—the two armies confronted each other in the field. The exact location of the battle is not known, but the encounter probably took the form of a running engagement southeast of Manzikert, across an arid plain that gives way to barren mountains about seven and a half miles away. The Byzantine army was deployed, as tradition demanded, along a straight front, with the emperor commanding the center. Behind him he had a strong rear guard commanded by Andronicus Ducas.

Alp Arslan chose to direct his forces from a distance—probably from the uplands on the edge of the plain, where the terrain was cut by ravines and gullies that made ideal hiding places for his reserves and ambushing units. He gave command in the field to a eunuch called Tarang, who formed the Seljuks into a crescent, their typical battle formation. Earlier, the sultan had laid aside his bow and arrow and taken up sword and mace, signaling to his men that this would be a battle to the death. Although the Byzantines could not know it, he was even less optimistic of his chances than they had deduced; he reportedly went into the battle wearing a white garment that could, if necessary, serve as his burial shroud.

To begin with, both sides maintained good order, the Byzantines advancing en masse, the Seljuks falling back in the center and harassing the enemy on the flanks. The sultan's camp was taken, empty and abandoned; Romanus pressed on. Apparently he was sweeping all before him, but in reality, by failing to force an engagement, he had lost all hope of winning a swift victory. The open terrain favored his opponents, and now the cavalry on his flanks, infuriated by the constant hail of arrows, broke away in pursuit and fell into an ambush. Still the emperor advanced, so frustrated at his inability to get to grips with the enemy that it was dusk before he realized his predicament. He was many miles away from his undefended camp, his men were weary and hungry, and his forces could be picked off piecemeal in the dark. There was only one action he could take. He ordered the imperial standard to be reversed, signaling a general retreat.

But in the failing light of evening, the cavalry on the wings misinterpreted the signal, imagining it to mean that the emperor had fallen. Watching the confusion from his high vantage, Alp Arslan ordered his Seljuks to wheel and attack; breaking through the right wing, they cut off the Byzantines' line of retreat. Even at that point, Romanus might have been saved if the rear guard had ridden to his aid, but Andronicus Ducas fled precipitously away, spreading the rumor that the emperor had been defeated. Other units were caught up in the panic and turned tail, while those that remained—including most of the mercenaries—either ignored the emperor's rallying call or simply did not know which way to turn. "It was like an earthquake," the soldier Attaleiates reported, "with howling, sweat, a swift rush of fear, clouds of dust, and not least hordes of Turks riding all around us. Depending on his speed, resolution, and strength, each man sought safety in flight. The enemy chased them, killing some, capturing some, and trampling others under their horses' hoofs. It was a terribly sad sight, beyond any lamenting or mourning. What could be more pitiable than seeing the entire imperial army in flight, defeated and chased by inhuman and cruel barbarians, the imperial tents, symbols of military might and sovereignty, taken over by men of that stripe, the whole Roman state overturned and knowing that the empire itself was on the verge of collapse?"

With only a handful of his personal guards at his side, Romanus made a last stand, fighting on with a head wound until his horse was brought down under him and he was made captive. Most of his army was cut down around him.

In victory, Alp Arslan was magnanimous. For eight days he kept Romanus as an honored guest while they discussed peace terms. The sultan could have dictated almost any conditions he wanted, but he had no wish for conquest in the west, preferring to keep Byzantium friendly, or at least neutral, while he pursued his war against the Fatimids in Egypt and North Africa. He knew, too, of the dissensions and rivalries in Constantinople. With that in mind, he decided to release the emperor with full honors in return for a large ransom, the restitution of frontier strongholds, the return of Muslim prisoners, the provision of Byzantine troops on demand, and most important, an alliance to be cemented by a marriage between the emperor's daughter and the sultan's eldest son.

Unfortunately, Romanus never had a chance to fulfill the agreement. When news of the disaster was brought to Constantinople by the traitor Andronicus, Romanus's stepson, Michael Ducas, had himself proclaimed emperor. Returning to find himself deposed, Romanus fought to regain his title but was defeated by Andronicus and obliged to give himself up under a promise of immunity guaranteed by the new emperor and three archbishops. Other elements, however, fearing that Romanus would mount another bid for the throne, had him blinded. A Byzantine historian described his fate: "Carried forth on a cheap beast of burden like a decaying corpse, his eyes gouged out and his face and head swollen and full of worms and stench, he lived on a few days in pain and smelling foully, and finally died."

Alp Arslan was furious when the news reached him. Declaring the treaty he had negotiated with Romanus void, he vowed to wage war on the "Roman atheists" and on all of Christendom. He was unable to take vengeance himself, however, for

The Seljuks' Courtly Rivals

While the Seljuks were carving out an empire in Iran and Iraq, their archrivals, the Fatimid rulers of Egypt, were creating one of the most refined civilizations of the Middle Ages. Among the artistic innovations that they encouraged was a new style of lusterware—a type of pottery first developed in Iraq in the ninth century. The plates and bowls that typify the ware were generally first covered with a white glaze, then painted with bright, metallic pigments, or lusters. The Fatimid vessels were distinguished by lively, figurative designs reflecting the lifestyle of the courtiers who would ultimately buy them.

trouble had flared on the other side of his empire, and the sultan was forced to hurry east to put down the rebellion. There, by a bizarre twist of fate, Alp Arslan met his own death at the hands of the commander of a fort he had captured. The prisoner, bound hand and foot, was brought before him and began to revile him, accusing him of cowardice. Incensed, Alp Arslan ordered the man to be released so that he could shoot him dead himself, but his arrow flew wide. In the ensuing confusion, the prisoner drew a concealed dagger and sprang at the sultan, stabbing him before he was himself hacked to pieces. Four days later, in November of 1072, the victor of Manzikert, conqueror of the Western world's greatest army, died of his wounds in distant central Asia.

The death of Alp Arslan brought Asia Minor no reprieve. With the Byzantine border-defense system shattered, Turkoman bands, owing allegiance only to their own chieftains, poured into the province. For decades past, such groups had raided the area, then departed; now, with no force to oppose them, they chose to remain. Christian mercenary bands, one of them led by the same Roussel of Bailleul who had abandoned Romanus before Manzikert, also sought to carve out territories for them-

selves. The result was a state of anarchy that the emperors in Constantinople did not even attempt to control.

The strongest leader to take advantage of the situation was Sulayman, a son of the Kutulmush who had vied for power with Alp Arslan in 1063. By birth, Sulayman may have belonged to the Seljuk ruling family, but in Asia Minor, he chose to operate on his own behalf. His ambition was to create a strong, independent sultanate, and in pursuing it, he was actively helped by the various court factions in Constantinople who, in the wake of Romanus's deposition, had lapsed into civil war. To further their personal ambitions, rival claimants for the Byzantine throne vied for Sulayman's military support, even though they knew that in so doing they were hastening the breakup of the empire. By 1078, Sulayman was in a position to proclaim himself sultan of Rum, recognizing only perfunctorily, if at all, the suzerainty of Alp Arslan's son Malik-Shah, who had succeeded his father as ruler of the Seljuk empire.

Unlike his father, Malik-Shah was not a Turk of the steppe by birth, and his name, combining the Arabic word for "king" with its Persian equivalent, signifies the Seljuk leader's desire to unite the entire Muslim East under the authority of a dynasty that would assimilate the culture of its subjects. The sultan continued to speak mainly

Two lusterware bowls feature exotic animals familiar to Fatimid courtiers. The cheetah, shown with its keeper (left), was used as a hunting animal, while the giraffe (right) would have formed part of the royal menagerie.

Turkish, however, and preserved the ancient Oghuz custom of sending an arrow with his dispatches as a symbol of his authority. The bow and arrow also feature in another persistent Seljuk tradition, the *tughra*. Originally, this was the brand mark by which nomad chieftains identified their livestock, but from Malik-Shah's reign it was used as a royal crest to authenticate documents. As a symbol of the authority of the sultans, it was to continue in use in the Turkish world for centuries to come.

The Seljuks' steppe-dwelling heritage also found expression for the nobility in their favorite pursuits of polo, hawking, and hunting. Malik-Shah was so devoted to the tracking down of game that he kept a record of his kills. (The biggest tally claimed for him and his entourage on any one day was a mind-boggling 10,000 beasts.) Nomadic traditions were also recalled in the Seljuks' palaces, which took the form of a number of detached pavilions and kiosks linked into an architectural whole by an encircling outer wall.

In other respects, however, the old Seljuk way of life was increasingly replaced by Persian, Arabic, and Byzantine influences. Although few details of his personal life are known, Malik-Shah was certainly a more urbane character than his great-uncle Tughril, who had probably never slept under a fixed roof in his life and who, when he first sampled almond confectionery, declared that it was delicious except for the omission of garlic.

Only eighteen years of age when he became sultan, Malik-Shah was still under the guardianship of Nizam al-Mulk when he came to the throne and never succeeded in throwing off the vizier's influence. Nizam al-Mulk devoted his great talents to strengthening the sultan's hand against his unruly followers by increasing the power of bureaucrats and palace officials—a system alien to the Seljuks, who traditionally shared their territorial conquests among the ruling family. The vizier set down his political theories in the *Siyasat-nama*, or *Book of Government*. Kings should keep their subjects "in such a position that they know their stations and never remove the ring of servitude in their ears," the vizier claimed. He also suggested that great commanders should be kept in their place by holding their sons hostage on a rotational basis, advised that the army should be composed of troops of different nationalities to reduce the risk of their forming alliances against their common master, emphasized the need for the sultan to impress his court by keeping a well-stocked table, and repeated the recommendation, turned down by Alp Arslan, that the court should be infiltrated by agents of the sultan. Severity toward disloyal subjects, he made clear, must be balanced by justice for the loyal.

However great Nizam al-Mulk's influence on the sultan himself may have been, he had limited means at hand to enforce his will on the empire as a whole. Nevertheless, he did what he could to further the establishment of centralized administration. In so doing, he also managed to advance many of his own friends and relatives, and he amassed such an enormous personal fortune that he became the object of much envy. A court jester in the sultan's entourage who was unwise enough to make jokes about the vizier's avaricious ways died after Nizam al-Mulk's followers seized him and ripped out his tongue.

Although the sultan occasionally showed his resentment of his chief minister's excesses by consulting other hostile advisers, he kept the vizier in power, and together they saw the Seljuk empire reach its peak. Malik-Shah's suzerainty was recognized in Mecca and Medina and down the Red Sea coast of Arabia; and in addition, he acquired a large part of Syria in 1086, when his brother defeated the rebellious Sulayman, whose sultanate of Rum now lost its eastern territories. Arriving to inspect his new possession, Malik-Shah led his horse to drink the water of the Mediterranean and gave thanks to Allah for allowing him to extend his dominions to the western sea.

For all the sultan's authority and his vizier's political astuteness, the real strength of the regime resided in the army. By the standard of the age, it was very large, including about 70,000 cavalry alone. In Alp Arslan's time, the army had consisted exclusively of Turkomans, but Malik-Shah, recognizing the threat these anarchic tribesmen posed to the stability of his empire, decided to keep them in check by building up a standing force of military slaves, or *mamluks,* who were loyal to his own person. Most mamluks were recruited from lands that were not monotheistic, so their enslavement was justifiable under the laws of Islam, but conversion to the faith of Muhammad was a condition of their training, and once this had been accomplished they were effectively emancipated and were not barred from holding even high office.

Loyal and well disciplined, many of the mamluks rose to senior military commands or provincial governorships. A favored few were appointed to the position of *atabeg,* a term meaning literally "father-chief." Such men were entrusted with the education and protection of young princes and in effect governed as regents until their wards came of age, so their trustworthiness had to be beyond question.

Although the standing force was sufficient for routine duties and small-scale operations, large military campaigns demanded the addition of auxiliary forces. The provision of these supplementary troops was the main obligation expected of the provincial governors, or emirs. In Malik-Shah's day, emirs were not allowed to own the lands they administered but in return for their services were granted an allocation of tax revenue known as the *iqta.*

Such a system impoverished many of the native landlords, but at least the troops they paid for guaranteed a peace in which trade could expand. Roads were improved and caravansaries built to provide for merchants who traveled from as far as the Hindu Kush and the shores of the Red Sea to trade in Baghdad and Basra, Nishapur and Herat. Since the Seljuk ruling family was itself foreign, poorly educated, and mostly involved with military affairs, the administration of the empire was left in the hands of a bureaucracy staffed almost entirely by Persians, who used their power to foster a revival of Persian language and culture from Asia Minor to northern India. The movement was encouraged by the vizier himself, a generous patron of learning as well as an outstanding statesman.

One of the brightest luminaries of this cultural efflorescence was the poet and

A Book of Verses underneath the Bough,
A Jug of Wine, a Loaf of Bread—and Thou
Beside me singing in the Wilderness—
Oh, Wilderness were Paradise enow!

One of Omar Khayyam's best-known rubaiyat, or quatrains, is complemented by a detail from an ivory plaque depicting a man quaffing wine and a musician playing a lute. A great mathematician as well as a poet, Khayyam was one of the brightest luminaries of a Persian intellectual world that at first felt threatened by its alien and unlettered Seljuk rulers, but that later flourished under the peace they imposed. Khayyam's verses show him to have been a pessimist who sought consolation for the fleetingness of human life in a hedonistic desire to enjoy each moment before it passes. Although he was employed by the Seljuk sultans as a court astronomer, he was too worldly and skeptical to sympathize with their strict enforcement of Islamic law—especially the stern prohibition of wine and drunkenness.

scientist Omar Khayyam. Born in about 1050, the son of a tentmaker, Khayyam distinguished himself at an early age as a brilliant mathematician. It was in this capacity that the vizier attached him to the court, where he completed a reform of the Persian solar calendar. He was also widely reputed for his skill in predicting future events. In the West, however, he would be best known for his rubaiyat, or quatrains, four-line poems that reveal a pessimistic view of life and a passionate philosophic concern with the nature of humanity's place in the universe.

Most of the artists and administrators of the time were graduates of madrasas—institutes of learning established to teach religion and science from an orthodox Sunni point of view. Similar institutions had existed for a century in Khurasan, the home state of Nizam al-Mulk, who recognized their value in countering Shiite propaganda. Staunch Sunnis themselves, the Seljuk rulers were easily persuaded to establish madrasas on an unprecedented scale. By making the best education available only to Sunni Muslims, who were then recruited to the most important positions in the fields of justice and administration and religion, the Seljuks dealt a serious blow to the adherents of the Shiite doctrines espoused by Fatimid Egypt.

The most famous of the madrasas, the Nizamiya, was founded in Baghdad by Nizam al-Mulk himself. Here he summoned the greatest scholars of the Muslim world, including the philosopher al-Ghazali, whose great work was to draw Sufism—Islam's mystical branch, which previously had been regarded as intellectually disreputable—into the mainstream of Islamic theology. For four years, al-Ghazali taught at the madrasa; the more he taught and the more he studied, however, the more he questioned whether reason alone could disclose the ultimate proof of God's existence. After a period of tormented doubt, he came upon the works of the Sufis, regarded at the time as at best zealots and at worst madmen for their antirational insistence on the importance of a direct, mystical comprehension of the presence of God. The result was a revelation; in his own words, al-Ghazali realized "that what is most distinctive of them can only be achieved by personal experience, ecstasy and a change of character." So in 1095, at the age of thirty-six, he gave up his prestigious position, disposed of his wealth, and retreated from public life on the pretext of making a pilgrimage to Mecca. In fact, he spent most of the next eleven years in Syria, undertaking a reexamination of his faith and writing works that reconciled the inner-directed and ecstatic approach of the Sufis with the orthodoxies of the established faith. According to an Islamic tradition, a "renewer" of religion is expected to appear at the beginning of each Islamic century. Convinced that this was his mission, al-Ghazali returned to teaching at the second madrasa to bear the name of his patron, the Nizamiyah at Nishapur. He continued to uphold the Sufi faith until his death in 1112, at the age of fifty-four.

Al-Ghazali's career demonstrated that the mysticism that appealed to the Islamic masses was not incompatible with the dogmatism of the orthodox hierarchy. But there could be no such accommodation with the Shiites. At the end of Malik-Shah's reign, they found a new champion in Hasan-i Sabbah, a man of impressive culture and deadly ruthlessness who legend would say had once been a friend of both Nizam al-Mulk and Omar Khayyam. Disillusioned with the emasculated Shiite movement in Egypt, Hasan severed connections with the Fatimids in Cairo and founded a new esoteric order devoted to furthering the Shiite cause by any means. To achieve his ends, he built up a small army of fanatical disciples to launch a terrorist campaign against the Sunni Seljuks, whom he regarded as the principle enemies of the Shia faith. Among the members of his order, the agents who carried out the political killings were called "Self-Sacrificers"; to orthodox Muslims, who believed that the murderers carried out their deeds under the influence of hashish, they were known as *hashishin*, a phrase later translated by Crusaders from the West as "Assassins."

In 1090, the Assassins seized the fortress of Alamut in the Elburz Mountains south of the Caspian Sea, and two years later, they claimed their first important victim—no less a figure than Nizam al-Mulk himself, who was stabbed to death while making his way to his harem tent by an Assassin disguised as a Sufi. There were rumors, however, that the murder had been ordered by Malik-Shah, who was becoming increasingly restive at his vizier's influence. If so, he did not profit by it, for he himself died of unknown causes in the same year.

"When Nizam al-Mulk was assassinated," wrote an Arab historian of the thirteenth century, "the state disintegrated." In the succession struggle that followed, the empire broke up into a mosaic of autonomous principalities, not all of them ruled by Turks. Disintegration was hastened by an extension of the iqta system, by which beneficiaries were assigned the control of entire provinces, with powers that made them almost independent of the central government. Atabegs took advantage of the disorder to usurp the powers and the estates of the princes entrusted to their care and set themselves up as hereditary rulers in their own right, while the Abbasid caliphs in Baghdad—who as spiritual overlords had to legitimize the succession—seized the chance to recover their political prestige by playing off one claimant against another.

The last of the Seljuk rulers of Iran died on the battlefield in 1194. Of the other Seljuk-ruled fragments of the eleventh-century empire, the most enduring was to be the sultanate of Rum, where the heirs of Sulayman profited from the chaos following Malik-Shah's death to reestablish their rule. For much of the twelfth century, the Seljuks of Rum bore the brunt of the fighting against the Crusader armies.

Rum, like the rest of the Seljuk world, finally fell to the Mongols in the thirteenth century. But by then, the Turkish presence in Asia Minor was firmly entrenched. That, finally, was to be the Seljuks' most enduring legacy. The Turkish peoples were never to leave the Anatolian plateau they had occupied within ten years of Alp Arslan's victory at Manzikert. It was the battle that created Turkey.

A CHALLENGE FROM THE CHURCH

In eleventh-century Europe, where much of life revolved around manual labor, warfare, and hunting, there was only one institution to which people could turn to find a deeper meaning in life: the Church. It was the guardian of high aspiration, the repository of spiritual truth. In practical terms, it had a virtual monopoly over education, running the only schools and possessing, in the libraries of its monasteries, most of the available books. Those few people who could read and write were almost invariably clergy; so when secular rulers sought administrators to prepare deeds or keep records, they turned to the Church.

More vitally yet, it was to the Church that all people, however mighty and powerful, looked for hope of salvation in the life to come. Even great sinners would find their thoughts turning toward it as the shadow of death, never far away in turbulent times, loomed close. Many kings and nobles sought to lighten their burden of sin by founding a church or abbey where prayers could be offered for their souls; others endowed existing institutions with an additional grant of land. In such ways, the Church had become over the centuries a great landowner, controlling estates as extensive and wealthy as those of the most powerful barons.

However great the Church's wealth and prestige might be, though, there were real limits to its power. It had blossomed and flourished through the grace and favor of the mighty, and in the long run, its position depended on their goodwill. In terms of brutal realism, the lay magnates had the weapons; and in troubled times, they could use them to enforce their wishes.

Such had been the case in the dark days of the ninth and tenth centuries, when the clergy had fallen increasingly under the con-

trol of local magnates; even the papacy itself was bought and sold among competing clans of the Roman nobility. Simony—the practice of purchasing Church office—was rife, and the quality of the priesthood was correspondingly low. Vows of chastity were often openly flouted, and many priests devoted more time to hunting than to caring for their flocks. The rot spread to the top: One tenth-century pope, John XII, was accused by hostile chroniclers of wrongdoings that included arson and fornication as well as castrating rivals and publicly drinking the health of the devil.

Yet even in the Church's blackest hours, the seeds of renovation were being sown. The dynamo of reform was the monastery of Cluny, founded in 910 in east-central France. Preaching a return to spiritual values, its monks spread their message across Europe, winning appointments to abbacies and bishoprics in many lands. By the start of the eleventh century, the abbot of Cluny ranked second in prestige only to the pope within the Catholic communion, with 300 monasteries under his control.

One reason for the Cluniacs' success was the encouragement they received from lay rulers and, in particular, from the greatest and most powerful of them all, the Holy Roman Emperors. Heirs to Charlemagne, the emperors boasted rights of overlordship in the patchwork of duchies, principalities, and urban communes that made up Germany, Italy, and surrounding lands. Ruling a realm that stretched from north of Hamburg to south of Rome, and from the Rhone River in France eastward to the borders of Hungary, they claimed the imperial mantle of the caesars.

Yet there were limits to their power too. Though generally selected on dynastic principles—an elder son of an emperor could normally expect to succeed his father—they had to go through the formality of election by the notables of the realm; they were then, by tradition, crowned by the pope. At times when the emperors were strong, election and coronation were simply rituals; but by the mid-eleventh century, voices were claiming that the papal crowning was no mere matter of form. The emperors were elected to fulfill a holy duty of serving the Church, some clerics held; in so doing, they were bound in fealty to its leader, the pope.

Such claims reflected a mood of self-confidence that would have been unthinkable a century earlier. In the Church's growing assertiveness lay the roots of a conflict that—enflamed by the stubbornness of two proud and headstrong men—was to ignite the bitter confrontation known as the Investiture Contest. The immediate quarrel was over the right to appoint clergymen; but behind it lay a deeper divide that amounted to no less than a rivalry for the ultimate leadership of Catholic Christendom.

The protagonists of this epic clash of wills were, on the one hand, the emperor Henry IV and, on the other, a zealous churchman of uncompromising character named Hildebrand. Born of poor parents near the Tuscan town of Sovana in 1020, Hildebrand had been educated at his uncle's monastery in Rome, where he had become a zealous supporter of the Cluniac movement. Contemporary sources describe him as short in stature, undignified in appearance, with a thin, reedy voice. What he lacked in physical presence, though, he made up in spiritual fervor, and he rose rapidly through the ecclesiastical ranks to become archdeacon of Rome. Elected pope in 1073 with the title of Gregory VII, he launched a reform program, deposing priests who had bought their offices and forbidding married clerics to celebrate Mass. More controversially, he announced that excommunication would be imposed on laymen who appointed clergy. This policy quickly brought him into conflict with the emperor, who had just come of age and was eager to assert his own will.

Thirty years younger than Gregory, Henry IV was a shrewd and opportunistic monarch who, according to his biographer, "perceived the workings of the mind of him upon whose face he cast the sharpness of his eyes; and he saw as though with lynxlike vision whether he carried toward him hate or love in his heart." Henry well knew that he could not afford to lose an effective voice in the selection of bishops, who besides being spiritual leaders were also important temporal lords. They were not only great landowners and feudal vassals of the king; they were also vital—

and inevitably highly political—agents in the civil government of the kingdom. Yet Gregory VII believed with equal conviction that it was imperative to deny that voice to the emperor or any other ruler, since experience taught that bishops appointed by lay magnates lacked both independence of action and the right qualities for spiritual leadership. The stage was set for a showdown.

The immediate point of dispute between the two men was the appointment of a new bishop to the important see of Milan. Henry, troubled by civil war in his German lands, at first judged it prudent to favor Gregory's candidate for the post. In 1075, however, when the strife seemed at an end, Henry executed an about-face, putting forward another candidate of his own choosing and personally investing his man with the ring and staff that symbolized holy office. Gregory regarded this action as a betrayal; he threatened the emperor with excommunication—a sentence that would cut Henry off from the consolations of the Church and would even challenge his legitimacy as a Christian ruler. In retaliation, Henry encouraged a group of German bishops to address a bitter letter to Hildebrand—"no longer pope, but false monk"—declaring him deposed. Gregory responded first by deposing the bishops and then by carrying out the threatened excommunication of Henry himself. By now, both parties were entrenched in positions that allowed no room for compromise.

At first, Gregory had support among the German princes. At a meeting with them, Henry was given to understand that if he failed to have the excommunication lifted within the year he would be deposed. Arrangements were made for a meeting in Augsburg, at which judgment would be pronounced on the emperor; Gregory was invited to attend. In the past, emperors had made and unmade popes; now the Church could return the favor.

Gregory set off from Rome with his staunch ally Countess Matilda of Tuscany to journey to Augsburg. He had not traveled far when he received momentous news; Henry had crossed the Alps and was advancing to meet him. Fearing for his life, the pope sought refuge in the countess's best-defended castle, Canossa in the Apennines. Ringed by triple walls, it was the strongest fortress of the region. There Gregory waited for the emperor's arrival.

When Henry duly appeared it transpired that Gregory's fears had been groundless. The emperor had realized that his position was politically untenable; without papal absolution he would lose his crown. So he had come, not to apprehend Gregory, but to beg his forgiveness. To plead his cause, Henry had brought his godfather, Abbot Hugh of Cluny, a friend of Gregory's, and one of the few men whose words might bear weight with the obdurate pope.

So was played out the most dramatic encounter of the century. For three January days, the most powerful monarch of the Western world stood barefoot in the snow within the second wall of the castle, wearing the coarse woolen tunic of a repentant sinner. Inside, Abbot Hugh besought Gregory to show mercy; and Countess Matilda added her voice to the plea for Christian charity.

Gregory knew that even in the moment of his triumph he was trapped. If he absolved Henry, he would in practice be restoring his sworn enemy to the imperial throne; yet as a man of God, he could not reject a penitent. Eventually, he yielded and granted the absolution that Henry sought. In return, Henry swore a solemn oath to grant the pope safe conduct to the Augsburg convocation and to accept the judgment that should be passed there.

The meeting was never to take place. When news of the absolution reached the German princes, they split into two factions. One renewed its allegiance to the emperor, now restored to the bosom of the Church. The other declared Henry deposed regardless of Gregory's act and proceeded to elect one of their own number, a prince named Rudolf of Rheinfelden, in his stead. Civil war raged for three years, while Gregory stood impatiently on the sidelines. Eventually, when the tide of battle began to turn in favor of Henry, the pope's gall at the prospect of seeing his old adversary restored to full imperial power overcame counsels of prudence, and once more, with all the solemnity of his office, he cast down the sentence of excommunication on the monarch.

If Gregory hoped to repeat his earlier victory, he was to be sadly deceived. Rudolf was defeated and killed shortly thereafter, and the princes no longer had the will, nor the means, to challenge Henry. The emperor had no need now to seek absolution; rather he sought to wipe out the memory of his humiliation at Canossa by setting up a rival pope and installing him in Gregory's place. In 1084, he succeeded in capturing Rome. Besieged in the Castel Sant' Angelo, Gregory escaped from his archenemy only by appealing to the Norman rulers of southern Italy for help. The Norman leader Robert Guiscard raised the siege and rescued him; but Guiscard's knights took the opportunity to sack the city, so alienating the local population that Gregory had for his own safety to accompany his deliverers back to their home territory. He was never again to see the city where he had made his career and which, above all others, he loved. He died the following year in Salerno, south of Naples, where his last words are said to have been, "I have loved righteousness and hated iniquity; therefore I die in exile." His enemy Henry survived him by twenty-one strife-torn years, finally dying, still excommunicate, in 1106.

The issue that had divided the two men continued to trouble the following generation, until a compromise solution was finally negotiated at the German town of Worms in 1122. By the terms of the concordat agreed there, bishops were in future to be elected by their cathedral chapters; although the emperor (or other secular overlord) could be present at the election, he lost the symbolic right to invest the incumbent with ring and staff. Once the bishop had been elected, however, he had then to do homage to the ruler for the feudal estates of the church he inherited.

This formula, which neatly separated the bishop's spiritual and temporal roles, provided a solution to the immediate problem of investiture. But the larger questions raised by the Church's new assertiveness remained, for Gregory's bold claims had permanently changed the balance of power between lay and spiritual authorities. He himself may in death have tasted the bitterness of defeat; but his legacy to the Church was to be an era of papal ascendancy that endured throughout the Middle Ages.

THE NORMAN CONQUESTS

3 In the early morning of Thursday, September 28, 1066, the inhabitants of Pevensey on the coast of southeast England witnessed an extraordinary sight. Seaward, belled out by the strong southerly wind, was a wall of sails—the familiar sheet sails of square-rigged, open-decked Viking raiding vessels. But the people bold enough to linger soon realized that this was no mere raid. The 700 ships slowly bearing toward them contained a veritable host of warriors and their grooms, attendants, servants, carpenters, and engineers. The fleet carried more than 7,000 men all together. It was the greatest armada of invasion to cross the English Channel since the Roman conquests more than a millennium before.

At its head, on board his flagship *Mora,* was William, thirty-eight years old, duke of Normandy, and claimant to the throne of England. By setting sail from his native France, he was putting his fortune to the supreme hazard, for he had no idea of the size or disposition of the force that would oppose him nor when he would meet it. The invasion was a typically bold stroke by a leader who embodied the spirit of the Norman people—descendants of Viking raiders who, having established for themselves the strongest state in northern France, were now turning their immense energy, ambition, and rapacity on the rest of Europe.

William's great gamble paid off. Within three months of landing at Pevensey, the victorious duke was to be crowned William I at Westminster Abbey in London, and although it would take him five more years to complete the conquest of England, the fate of the ancient island kingdom was already sealed, having been settled by William's decisive victory at the Battle of Hastings. The Normans subsequently imposed a new ruling class on the Church and the State, fundamentally influenced the nation's government and law, strengthened the monarchy, revitalized the Church, constructed imposing castles and cathedrals, and not the least, severed England's long-established and uneasy ties with Scandinavia, which under the Danish king Cnut had for a short time provided the country's ruling dynasty. The Norman Conquest marked the birth of a new England.

In terms of world history, however, the conquest represents only part of the Norman achievement. Half a century before William crossed the Channel, Norman knights had started to make forays into southern Italy. By 1061, they dominated the area; and in that year, they assembled a 2,000-strong army to cross the narrow Strait of Messina and successfully challenge the might of the Saracens who had held Sicily under Islamic rule for more than two centuries. Carried out by free-lance knights in search of land and glory, this conquest was in some ways more impressive in its long-term effects than that of England. The conquest of Sicily led to the creation of the strongest monarchy in Europe and to the emergence of the most enlightened Christian kingdom of the Middle Ages: a rich, well-ordered period in which for the

In a detail from the 900-year-old Bayeux tapestry, three Norman knights raise arms to charge the Anglo-Saxon line during the Battle of Hastings—the decisive victory by which Duke William of Normandy won the English crown in 1066. This vast, multicolored work—not strictly a tapestry but a band of linen embroidered with woolen thread—presents a unique visual record of the events surrounding the Norman invasion.

first and last time in history the three great Mediterranean civilizations—Latin, Greek, and Arab—flourished side by side in relative harmony. By the end of the century, the son of Sicily's conqueror had further extended the Norman conquests to the shores of the Levant by establishing the principality of Antioch, which was among the earliest fruits of the victorious First Crusade.

Considering the impact they were to have, the Normans had behind them a relatively short history in the year 1000. Their name derives from "Norsemen," in reference to their Viking origin. More specifically, however, the word "Normans" meant those mainly Danish colonists who, in the mid-ninth century, had established permanent settlements on the French coast. Eventually they came to terms with Charles the Simple, king of the West Franks. In 911, he bought off their leader Rolf with the duchy of Normandy, a territory surrounding the lower river Seine, in return for an oath of allegiance and a promise to accept Christianity.

At that time, the West Frankish kingdom was made up of a small royal domain, centered in the Paris region, and a cluster of vassal states, which included the large duchies of Burgundy and Aquitaine, as well as smaller counties such as Brittany, Poitou, and Anjou. Outside the royal domain, the Frankish kings of the Capetian dynasty (so-called from its founder, Hugh Capet, who ascended the throne in 987)

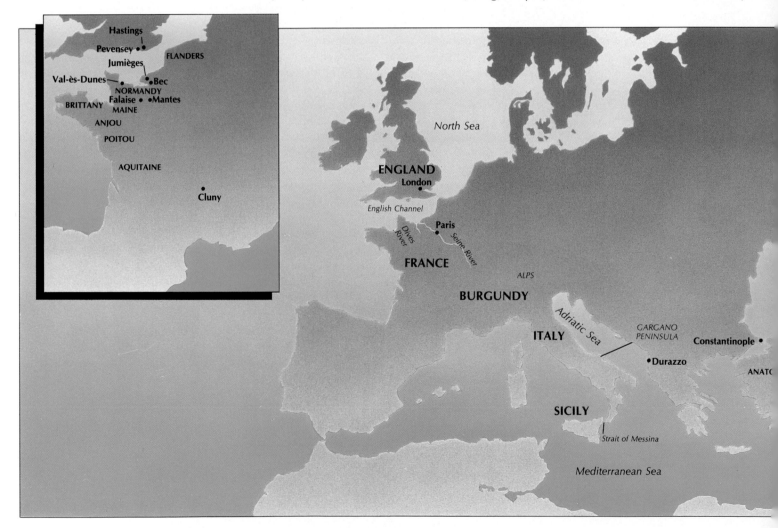

exerted little direct authority. Real power lay in the hands of the regional lords, who, while acknowledging the monarch in Paris as their nominal overlord, governed their lands as virtually independent rulers and conducted incessant wars against their neighbors. The Normans thrived under these turbulent conditions, and the new duchy quickly expanded. Eventually it formed a rough rectangle of primarily flat or gently rolling countryside extending more than 150 miles inland from the northwestern coast of France.

Within three generations, the newly founded duchy was to become the strongest of all the principalities in France. The reason for this astonishing progress was the ability and the willingness of the Normans to assimilate: to adopt existing institutions and systems, and then modify, strengthen, and improve them. Because the Normans were relatively few in number, they had to seek wives among their Frankish neighbors, embracing the Frankish language with such wholeheartedness that within a century the old Norse tongue had completely died out in France, leaving only vestigial traces in the local dialect.

During the same period, the Normans transformed themselves from heathen barbarians into devout, though at first not totally converted, Christians: Rolf's death was celebrated by gifts to monasteries to ensure the repose of his soul but also by a pagan blood sacrifice of 100 captives. Yet a century later, the Normans' devotion to their new religion was so great that they made up a major part of the travelers thronging the pilgrim roads to Rome and the Holy Land.

With the enthusiasm of the recently converted, they expanded and revitalized the Church in their lands, restoring destroyed dioceses and raising cathedrals and abbeys. The ecclesiastical revival that they initiated spread into the world of learning, and from the monasteries sprang great schools, such as the one founded in 1045 at the Abbey of Bec, in present-day Le Bec Hallouin, near Brionne, which drew pupils from all over western Europe.

Besides embracing the language and religion of their adopted homeland, the Normans studied Frankish military methods, which relied not on the warships familiar to the Vikings, but on land-based tactics, particularly the deadly combination of war-horse and lance. Protected by mail armor and firmly secured in the saddle by a combination of long stirrup leathers and an almost straight-legged riding posture, Norman knights at full gallop were a formidable force. A Byzantine observer, seeing them in action in the Crusades, would say half admiringly that such men could pierce the walls of Babylon.

The mounted warriors came to form both a military and a social elite. All the leading secular figures of the duchy were knights, an accolade only bestowed after an expensive and demanding apprenticeship to arms. However, not all knights were born wealthy: Because the Normans were by this time starting to follow the law of primogeniture, by which a dead man's estates normally passed intact to the first-born male heir, younger sons could only hope to gain land (and thus financial security) by giving distinguished service to a lord, who might reward them with estates granted out of his own territories or those of defeated enemies. Not all knights had such good fortune; many remained landless throughout their lives.

In theory, the ultimate owner of the land was, however, the reigning duke of Normandy, who granted it to his vassal lords only in return for the fulfillment of military obligations. The great majority of Norman barons, all the bishops, and many of the monasteries held tenure on condition that they maintained a specified number

Starting from their homeland in northwest France, the Normans in the course of the eleventh century created a piecemeal empire incorporating lands from the North Sea to the Mediterranean. Freebooting knights led the way, initially as mercenaries fighting for feuding Lombards and Greeks in southern Italy. By 1061, five years before Duke William's invasion of England, they had conquered most of southern Italy and had invaded Muslim-ruled Sicily. Subsequently, the knights seized the Greek island of Corfu and invaded the Balkan lands of the Byzantine Empire. During the First Crusade in 1098, they established the principality of Antioch.

of knights fully trained and equipped and ready for service as and when the duke had need of them. In this way the Norman dukes shaped an aristocracy that would serve their own interests.

Elsewhere in France and western Europe, similar feudal arrangements prevailed. Normandy, however, exceeded all other Frankish principalities in the rigor with which the obligations were enforced and the amount of attention devoted to the training and equipping of its army. To reduce the risk of baronial revolts, the Norman dukes stipulated that castles could only be built by ducal license and must open their gates to the duke and his men on demand. They also took pains to ensure that their own personal army was the largest in the duchy and met the expense of maintaining it by monopolizing the coinage and tolls on trade as well as through the feudal dues they received from their vassals and the proceeds of administering justice. To make sure their ducal rights were not abused, they appointed viscounts, answering directly to themselves, to collect revenues and be responsible for maintaining law and order. By such means the Norman dukes came to exert tighter control over their subjects than any other western European rulers of the time.

Under these circumstances, the success of Normandy as an efficient, unified state depended to a dangerous degree on the strength and character of its ruler. From 1028 to 1035, the duchy suffered ruthless subjugation by a man of rather too much strength and too little character, Duke Robert I, who came to power by having his elder brother killed and confining the dead man's son and heir to a monastery. To the horror of ecclesiastical chroniclers, he secured his position by giving away lands that belonged to the Church to vassals in return for their support. Normandy endured his excesses; but when he died of unknown causes in faraway Anatolia, while returning from a pilgrimage of penance to Jerusalem, the duchy was thrown into a state of anarchy. For Robert had never married, and his heir was a bastard son, William, who was an eight-year-old child.

William was the product of Robert's youthful dalliance with Herlève, the comely daughter of a tanner in the town of Falaise. On succeeding to the dukedom, Robert had not sought to legitimize the child by marrying the peasant girl in the Christian manner. Instead, after she had borne him a daughter, he married her off to a wealthy aristocrat, Herlwin de Conteville, by whom she had two sons, Odo and Robert. Three decades later when William conquered England, his young half-brothers—Odo, bishop of Bayeux, and Robert, count of Mortain—would be his principal lieutenants and among the chief beneficiaries of the conquest.

Such future glory, however, was beyond imagination during the turbulent years of William's minority. Indeed, it was a miracle that he survived to achieve manhood. Although he had the support of his feudal overlord, the West Frankish king Henry, his succession was disputed, thereby signaling the collapse of central authority. In the ensuing decade of anarchy barons, great and small, assumed local independence, extorting taxes for their own profit and assembling armies to fight their own wars. William owed his survival to the support of a loyal faction among the barons. Nonetheless, he was the target of at least one murder attempt, which he only escaped thanks to advance warning and a dramatic night flight back to his castle at Falaise. In addition, three of his guardians were assassinated during this time of turmoil: Both his tutor and seneschal died violent deaths; and his uncle Osbern was killed in a struggle when rebels penetrated the boy duke's chamber.

In a page from an illuminated Anglo-Saxon manuscript, Saint John the Evangelist, penning his gospel, looks up for inspiration toward a symbolic eagle clutching a horn. The document, known as the Grimbald Gospels, dates from the early eleventh century and was the work of a monk of Canterbury, in southeastern England. Rich in imagery and innovative in design, it bears witness to the advanced artistic traditions of Anglo-Saxon England before the Norman Conquest.

From humble wayside chapels to great cathedrals, the churches erected in great numbers throughout Europe in the eleventh century demonstrated a new architectural manner that combined local traditions with Roman and Byzantine influences. As great builders, the Normans were to play an important part in spreading this Romanesque style throughout the lands they conquered.

As the French examples shown here suggest, the strength of Romanesque buildings derived from their massive walls, usually made of rubble bound by mortar and faced with flat stones. The space inside these walls was divided by sturdy columns and wide semicircular arches on the Roman model; the arches' shape was echoed by the vaulted roofs. Decorative details were limited to a few key points—the capital stones at the top of columns or the recessed arches above doorways—and the overall effect was one of tranquil majesty.

During the second half of the twelfth century, the use of buttresses to support the weight of the vaulted roofs obviated the need for such thick walls, and the Romanesque style of architecture began to give way to the Gothic.

Human and animal faces stare impassively from the top of a column in the church of Anzy-le-Duc in the upper Loire valley in France. Such decorative carvings often featured Christian religious themes, but many showed the influence of Celtic or ancient Middle-Eastern art.

Sunlight entering through the narrow windows of Anzy-le-Duc spotlights the decorated capitals that separate the tall stone columns and the arches they support.

A series of groin vaults—formed by the intersection of semicircular barrel vaults—provides a treelike roof at the abbey of Silvacane in Provence. Early Romanesque builders constructed such vaults for adornment over a temporary framework of timber; later, the arched ribs were built first, to provide support, and the spaces between them were then filled with stone vaulting.

The vaulting of the nave of the abbey church of Saint-Philibert on the Saône River rests on arches built of contrasting brick and stone. Windows, arches, and vaults all contribute to an echoing sequence of semicircles.

It was Normandy's good fortune that the young duke grew strong in body and steely in character, and that by the age of sixteen, he had become sufficiently proficient in the arts of combat to be knighted by King Henry. Three years later, in 1047, he successfully crushed an army commanded by his cousin and rival, Guy of Burgundy, who also laid claim to the dukedom. This battle, fought at Val-ès-Dunes on the wide plain west of Caen, marked the beginning of William's personal ascendancy. His conduct in the battle was impressive; one chronicler, noting that "the greater part of the Normans fought under the banner of iniquity," added that William, "chief of the avenging host, was undismayed by the sight of their swords; hurling himself upon his enemies, he terrified them with slaughter." He subsequently displayed political acumen, too, in pardoning all but one of the surviving rebel barons in exchange for their sworn allegiance.

This was not the end of the infighting in Normandy, but with each succeeding year William tightened his grip upon his inheritance. He also secured his borders against outside attack. In 1048, he joined with King Henry to defeat Geoffrey Martel of Anjou, who threatened his southern frontier. Some three years later, he married Matilda, the diminutive four-foot-tall daughter of Baldwin of Flanders, whose land lay to the northeast of Normandy. The match proved happy and fruitful: The couple had at least five daughters and four sons, two of whom—William and Henry—were destined to become kings of England.

The Flanders marriage increased William's power to such a worrying extent that his longtime supporter King Henry turned against him. Forging an alliance with Geoffrey Martel, the king invaded Normandy in 1054 and again in 1058. Each time William's tactical skill won the day, and the invaders were forced to withdraw after suffering heavy losses. When both Henry and Geoffrey died in 1060, their successors decided to abandon these fruitless raids. William could now afford to take the offensive, which he did with spectacular success, conquering the neighboring county of Maine in 1063 and, the following year, marching westward to impose his suzerainty on the duchy of Brittany.

Duke William was now the most powerful ruler in northern France, controlling territory that stretched from Mont-Saint-Michel in the west as far as the Île-de-France. Gone were the days when recalcitrant subjects dared taunt the young duke by beating skins and shouting, "Hides for the tanner." William was now feared and respected by the overwhelming majority of his people.

The benefits of his sternly capable leadership were there for all to see: a highly efficient ducal administration, a flourishing, revitalized Church, and growing prosperity. Like most of the feudal princes of his time, William was almost certainly illiterate. But his early life had made him a pragmatist, full of understanding and quick to adapt to prevailing circumstances and turn them to his own advantage. He was also a great champion of the Church and sincerely religious.

In person, he was tall and burly, though abstemious with food and drink. Contemporary chroniclers noted that, unusually for the time, he was both devoted and faithful to his wife. In speech he was fluent and persuasive, though harsh in his manner when he considered it necessary and violent when thwarted.

Above all, however, William was like most Norman lords a man of action, a lover of combat and hunting. By 1066, he had already spent almost all his life either preparing for or else engaged in war. Soldiering was—as society demanded—his natural profession as a ruler. And that year, with Normandy's position further secured by the outbreak of civil strife in neighboring Anjou, he was to have a momentous opportunity to exercise his calling, when the death of an heirless king enabled him to exert a longstanding claim to the English throne.

Less than 100 miles across the English Channel from Normandy, Anglo-Saxon England was a completely different world. Its ruler in the mid-eleventh century was King Edward, who was known as the Confessor for his piety. Edward was related through his mother to the Norman ducal family and had spent most of his youth and young manhood—the years of Cnut's reign in England—in exile at the Norman court. In 1051, nine years after his accession to the throne of England, he had named William, duke of Normandy, as his heir. This was the claim that William sought to assert on Edward's death in 1066.

He was not the only contender. King Harold Hardrada of Norway, the most renowned Viking warrior of his age, was seeking to reassert the Scandinavian title to the throne established earlier in the century by King Cnut. And in England itself, Harold Godwinson, earl of Wessex and the most powerful magnate in the land, also sought the supreme office, basing his claim on a supposed deathbed bequest by Edward and on the support of the royal council known as the witan. On Edward's death, he had the advantage of propinquity. Taking decisive action, he had himself crowned King Harold II of England in London's newly consecrated Westminster Abbey only hours after the dead king had been buried in the same church.

Harold's action was all the more galling to William because of an incident that had occurred two years earlier. At that time, Harold had appeared at the Norman court and had confirmed William's right to the English throne by swearing to it upon holy relics. Much controversy would surround this visit: Norman sources would insist that Harold arrived on an official mission, whereas Harold's supporters would maintain in contrast that he came to Normandy only as the result of a shipwreck and that the oath was sworn under duress. Whatever the truth of the matter, William exploited the story of Harold's perjury to good effect to obtain the support of the papacy for his own claim. With Pope Alexander II's blessing and the three-tailed papal banner to march under, his cause took on the aura of a holy war. Knightly volunteers surged into Normandy from all the principalities of northern France to swell his forces.

Within a few months, William succeeded in welding his Norman contingents and the foreign auxiliaries into a disciplined, cohesive fighting body. He ensured that his new army was properly quartered, equipped, and provisioned for a long campaign. At the same time, he set a vast labor force to work felling trees throughout the duchy and hauling timber to Normandy's ports. There shipwrights built literally hundreds of fifty-foot-long open-decked boats for the cross-Channel transport of the invading army and their thousands of horses. All this was achieved by early August 1066, when the fleet assembled in the estuary of the Dives River, 12 miles northeast of Caen and about 100 miles due south of England's Sussex coast.

A sinister portent had already aroused apprehension among the people of England. Earlier in that year, they had looked up in amazement as, on seven successive nights, a brilliant orb blazed a fiery trail across the heavens. The phenomenon would be identified centuries later as Halley's Comet. In 1066, it was generally considered to be an omen of doom.

Harold, however, did not need a comet to alert him to the threat of invasion. There was regular traffic between England and France, and returning travelers must have

Norman knights were armed and equipped in a manner artfully designed to give a high degree of protection while allowing maximum maneuverability on horseback. Their main body defense was the hauberk, a knee-length garment composed of interlinked metal rings. This flexible armor usually had short sleeves that left the forearms free and a skirt slit at the front and back to facilitate riding. The hauberk was normally extended into a coif, or hood, fitting over the head, which in any event was protected by a sturdy conical helmet sometimes beaten from a single piece of iron, with a separate iron strip riveted to its front rim as a noseguard.

Not all the body was armored. The hands were left bare, and the feet were covered by plain leather shoes over which were strapped spurs. Most knights wore only their tunics, shirts, breeches, and leggings beneath their hauberks, although all probably had some form of padding to protect their bodies from the chafing mail. Wealthier warriors (far left) might wear special mail leggings called chausses, as well as sleeves of mail to guard their forearms.

Fighting equipment was equally well suited to the demands of eleventh-century warfare. The long lance with a leaf-shaped metal tip was light enough to double as a javelin; once it was dispatched, the knight was free to draw his broad-bladed sword. The round-topped shield was secured by a loose strap around the warrior's neck and could be grasped by means of tighter thongs fixed inside it. The tapering shape served to guard the knight's legs without rubbing against his mount's flank.

warned him of the preparations under way in the Normandy ports. In anticipation, he had raised the greatest army and fleet that England had ever known. His army was composed of two kinds of men—the housecarls, an elite corps of professional soldiers comprising the retainers of his own household and of those of the earls and other great lords, and the fyrd, a national militia of freemen liable for conscription in time of danger. His fleet seems to have been composed mainly of ships requisitioned from merchants, used to transport troops according to strategic needs. At this time in western Europe, major sea battles were virtually unknown, except between galleys in the sheltered waters of the Mediterranean, because ships were so dependent for mobility on favorable winds that it was difficult for two fleets to become engaged from opposite directions.

Through most of July and all of August, Harold kept his forces at battle stations along the south coast; he himself commanded the fleet from the Isle of Wight. By mid-August, both armies were fully battle ready; but William's men were forced to kill time waiting for the south wind they needed to carry them across the Channel. To a degree, the unusually capricious nature of the winds that summer were to decide the fate of Anglo-Saxon England.

By early September, Harold no longer had sufficient provisions to maintain his militia on permanent duty. He disbanded the fyrd to allow the men to bring in their harvests before the crops were wasted. He himself returned with his housecarls to London. He ordered the fleet to make their way around the coast to the Thames River for a refit; many were wrecked en route by storms.

The unseasonably bad weather also affected the Norman fleet. Soon after Harold's departure, a brief south wind tempted their ships out to sea from the mouth of the Dives River. Historians disagree about the intended destination; some believe that the boats were headed for England, while others insist that William's plan was simply to move them up the coast to a more strategic location for a later invasion. In any event, westward-veering winds drove them up the Channel to the mouth of the Somme River. The projected Channel crossing was consequently reduced by almost half— from about a hundred miles to fifty-five. In the process, however, the Normans also lost a fair number of their ships.

About this time, Harold received news that a huge invasion force led by his other rival, King Harold Hardrada, had not merely set sail but had effected a landing 220 miles away in northeast England and had burned the ancient town of Scarborough to the ground. Aided by the predominantly northerly winds that had kept the Normans locked on the French coast, the Norwegians had crossed the North Sea with more than 200 longships and perhaps as many as 1,800 men. They were now ravaging the countryside and rapidly advancing on York, the capital of Northumbria.

King Harold reacted swiftly. At once, he mobilized his housecarls and rapidly recalled all the militia of southern England. Then, on about September 18, he began the long march north, strengthening his army along the way with the militia assembled in the eastern shires by his brothers Gryth and Leofwine. King Harold drove his army hard, and although he was unable to save York, he arrived sooner than the Norwegians anticipated. He had the advantage of surprise when, on September 25, he attacked the Norwegian encampment at Stamford Bridge, less than ten miles northeast of York. The battle was hard fought, raging from dawn to dusk, but by the end of the day the English forces had achieved an overwhelming victory, and Harold Hardrada lay among the dead.

In the shallows of Pevensey lagoon on the southeast coast of England, a Norman invasion force of at least 7,000 men disembarks from the armada of some 700 vessels that has carried it from Normandy. The operation was a nightmare of logistics. Some 3,000 cavalry mounts had to be unloaded from their makeshift stalls of wattle by way of ramps. The invaders also had to bring ashore cartloads of arms and armor, as well as other essential supplies ranging from tools and planks for building fortifications to cooking pots and barrels of wine. Providentially, the landing was unopposed, because the English army had been diverted by a Norwegian invasion in the north; the Normans were consequently able to establish a secure beachhead without the loss of a single life.

Generously, Harold allowed the few Norwegian survivors to return home in their thirty-four remaining ships, under oath that they would never attack England again. Ironically, they had little trouble on their journey, for as soon as they put to sea their sails were filled by a fresh breeze blowing, for the first time in two months, consistently from the south.

It was the wind that William's fleet had been waiting for. Harold had little time in which to celebrate the victory at Stamford Bridge. At the start of October, he received news that the Normans had landed at Pevensey and were laying waste to the Sussex coast. Without giving his battle-weary and footsore troops any time to rest, Harold led them by forced marches to London, where he paused to gather reinforcements before hurrying his army south. He reached Sussex on the night of October 13, having covered more than 430 miles in less than a month.

The next morning, when their respective trumpeters sounded the commencement of battle, the two armies stood just 220 yards apart, separated by a narrow valley about six miles inland from the port of Hastings. King Harold's troops, occupying the high ground, were drawn up on a defensive front extending perhaps some 650 yards along the ridge of the hill. Duke William's men were ranged along the foot of the rise and disposed in three divisions—on the left, a predominantly Breton force led by Count Alan of Brittany, in the center, the Normans under Duke William, and on the right, French, Flemish, and other mercenaries.

In some respects the two armies could scarcely have been more evenly matched. Both sides numbered an estimated 7,000 fighting men. Both the Saxon housecarls and the Norman knights—elite forces perhaps 2,000 strong—wore knee-length mail armor and carried kite-shaped shields. Both armies had archers in leather jerkins and foot soldiers armed with similar swords, spears, and daggers, although the invaders had a far greater number of the bowmen. On the other hand, the Saxon housecarls had a superior weapon in the five-foot-long double-edged ax, which could be swung with deadly effect to cut down man or horse.

Unlike the Anglo-Saxons, who fought entirely on foot, the Norman knights went into battle on horseback—although the advantage they gained in mobility was for much of the contest reduced by the terrain, a boggy valley and rising slopes that reduced the impact of the charge. Otherwise, the most visible difference between the opposing forces was the look of the soldiers. The Saxons were long-haired and often mustached, while the Normans had such short-cropped hair that many people of Sussex had initially thought that they had been invaded by an army of monks.

King Harold had chosen an admirable defensive position well suited to the Old English military tactics of standing and fighting. But he had perhaps made a mistake in offering battle so hastily, while his men were tired and

Time and distance were key factors in the Norman Conquest of England. When their fleet landed at Pevensey, King Harold's Anglo-Saxon army was in York, more than 200 miles away to the north, celebrating a famous victory over Norwegian invaders at the battle of Stamford Bridge. The English army marched back by way of London, meeting the invaders near Hastings less than three weeks after the earlier battle. Despite the decisive nature of the Norman victory, it was five years before England was subjugated. The Normans faced numerous rebel forces, notably in Yorkshire and on the Isle of Ely in the east of the country. Finally, in 1072, they secured the northern border by an attack on Scotland.

before the odds were weighed fully in their favor. His brother Gryth and other counselors had recommended that, rather than facing up to the invaders at once, he should lay waste to the countryside north of Hastings, so denying the invaders fresh supplies; at the same time he would buy time for his army to be strengthened by the reassembled northern fyrd of Earls Edwin and Morcar, and by new recruits from the west. If in the meantime William came out on the offensive, the counselors argued, the Anglo-Saxons would have the advantage of familiarity with the countryside in organizing ambushes and guerrilla-style raids. Being on home ground, in a country with a population of about 1.5 million people, the English could only become stronger, while the Normans would inevitably become weaker.

Duke William, however, gambled on the probability that King Harold would engage him as soon as possible in a decisive battle, and he was proved right. Harold proudly refused to delay in engaging an army that was ruthlessly ravaging the lands of his old earldom of Wessex. Perhaps, too, he believed that he could repeat the simple, resolute maneuver that had served him so well at Stamford Bridge—a long march followed by a quick thrust at the enemy before they were fully on guard. Instead, in the early morning of October 14, he found that the Normans, alerted by their mounted reconnaissance, were advancing in full strength to meet him.

Harold thereupon reverted to a more orthodox plan of battle. On the higher ground, his army formed the traditional Anglo-Saxon shield wall, a single block of men nine or ten ranks deep, with his mail-clad housecarls making up the front rank and standing thickest around the king in the center. Across the valley, Duke William's forces were deployed so that three different categories of troops—archers, infantry, and finally the squadrons of mounted knights—would be able to strike, one after another, in quick rotation.

William's first three-wave attack failed. His archers unleashed a succession of volleys, only to see most of their metal-tipped arrows bounce off the wall of shields. In contrast, a fusillade of English javelins, hand-axes, and stone hammers rained down with considerable effect on the Norman infantry, who advanced as the archers fell back. After a grim melee of hand-to-hand fighting, the infantry made way for the mounted knights to charge through any gaps that had been forced in the English line. But there were no gaps; the shield wall had held firm.

Amid the confusion of battle, a false rumor spread in the French ranks that the duke had been killed. Disheartened, the Bretons of Duke William's left flank began to give way down the hill. The opposing Saxon fyrd, believing that they had won the day, at once broke ranks to charge after them. In so doing, they weakened the western end of the Saxon line and exposed themselves to counterattack in the valley.

It was a critical point in the struggle, and Duke William himself did much to save the day. To prevent panic from spreading into the other divisions, he rode into the middle of the fray, rallied the Norman infantry in the center, and ordered his knights to wheel left and isolate the pursuing fyrdmen. Then, with discipline restored, he resumed his original tactics, launching repeated attacks by archers, infantry, and cavalry in swift succession.

For many hours, the battle raged without either side gaining a significant advantage and without any sign of the shield wall breaking. Then William, remembering the fyrdmen's error, ordered his knights to simulate a retreat—a common tactic in continental warfare, but one that may have been unfamiliar to the Anglo-Saxons. Again the undisciplined peasant-warriors of the fyrd charged downhill in pursuit of the fleeing Normans. It was a fatal mistake; at a given order the cavalry wheeled and cut down their pursuers. The Anglo-Saxon army suffered major losses, and the defensive line was considerably weakened.

Not long afterward, as evening approached, the Conqueror launched a general assault by all three arms; according to later accounts, he ordered his archers to fire on a high trajectory, so that their arrows would fall on the English from above rather than striking their shields. In the end, the wall of shields was penetrated, even to the royal headquarters in the center. Harold himself was struck by an arrow above the right eye and then was quickly cut down by eager Norman knights. With the death of the king, the English army broke, its remnants melting away into the gathering dusk of the broken countryside, ruthlessly pursued by the Norman horsemen. They left behind them on the field of battle the fallen flower of the kingdom's nobility and youth; on it the Conqueror was later to found Battle Abbey for the Benedictines in munificent penance for the slaughter. In the meantime, the decisive victory he had sought and prayed for had been won.

Within a week of victory, William had secured all the major ports of southeast England and was able to bring in reinforcements from Normandy. He then set about isolating London, which was too large and threatening a stronghold for him to take by force. His strategy was successful; by late December, all fighting in the southeast was ended as groups of English magnates—most notably the northern earls Edwin and Morcar, and two archbishops, Stigand of Canterbury and Eldred of York—formally surrendered the kingdom and invited Duke William to accept the crown.

This gesture, however, had limited meaning in a land so deeply governed by provincial loyalties. Another five years of bloody conflict and rebellion would pass before the Norman Conquest was complete. The gravest threat to William's rule came in the summer of 1069, when Danish invaders joined forces with the predominantly Scandinavian people of the northeast and soundly defeated the Normans at York. When the Danes returned with the spoils of victory to their longboats, William took a terrible revenge on the allies they left behind. In the two months leading up to Christmas, 1069, his soldiers spread havoc through the land between York and Durham, killing rebels and civilians alike and burning their crops and homes. Fifty years later a bishop of Durham would write of the famine, plague, and cannibalism that followed William's butchery, wiping out most of the inhabitants of the area. Thus William created a northern wasteland that would never again be able to support a major rebellion against his authority.

The last resistance came from south of the Humber River, where a Lincolnshire landowner called Hereward, surnamed the Wake, staged the final noteworthy challenge to William's rule. Supported by Danish invaders, he and his followers sacked the town of Peterborough in 1070. Once more, however, the Danes—satisfied with their plunder—left their allies, and the weakened force took refuge in a fortified camp on the Isle of Ely, deep in the marshy fenland of Cambridgeshire. There they held out for almost a year. When the rebel garrison was eventually overwhelmed, Hereward managed to escape and continued the struggle as an outlaw whose fame is remembered in England even today.

The northern frontier was secured by an invasion of Scotland in 1072, and the Norman triumph was complete. Thereafter, William chose to spend the greater part of his reign in his native Normandy, leaving the administra-   tion of England to regents, most of them churchmen, including Lanfranc, a   personal friend

The bodies of dead knights, shown in a detail from the border of the Bayeux tapestry, evince the carnage wreaked in the day-long Battle of Hastings. Few prisoners were taken in the conflict, which climaxed in a melee of cutting, hacking, and stabbing with swords and spears. Decapitation was a common fate for victims of the Anglo-Saxons' deadly five-foot-long battle-axes.

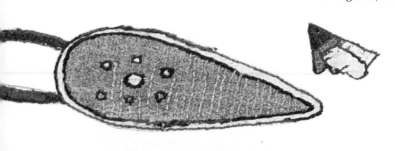
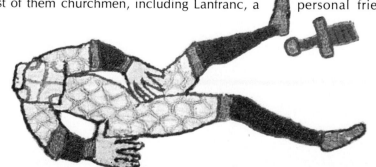

of William's and a former monk of Bec, who replaced Stigand as archbishop of Canterbury. Yet the Conqueror was allowed little tranquillity. He was obliged to return to England in 1075, following an attempted coup by the earls of Hereford and Norfolk, and again in 1085, when England was threatened for the last time by a Danish invasion. Otherwise, his time was taken up in defending Normandy's frontiers against invasion from hostile neighbors. In addition, he had to deal with a series of uprisings led by his eldest son, Robert, who bitterly resented his father's refusal to let him take any active part in the government of Normandy, which had nominally been handed over to him in 1066. So great was the threat to his duchy that William was compelled to ship contingents of the English fyrd across the Channel to fight alongside his barons and their knights.

By 1085, King William's resources were stretched so thin that he sought a means of establishing the true military capacity and taxable value of his English kingdom. To achieve this end, he ordered an economic survey of the country, intended to determine lordship, tenure, and value of property in every manor and village, however small. It was a national undertaking on a scale unparalleled for centuries to come, providing such a comprehensive record of England's resources that the king could tell exactly what taxes might be demanded of each district and how many men might realistically be called into military service. Recognizing the sinister fiscal implications of the survey, the English people equated it with the Day of Judgment. And so the name "Domesday" came to be given to the two Latin volumes that recorded the findings of the survey.

The *Domesday Book* was to provide graphic evidence of the speed and thoroughness with which William had swept away the old English order and replaced it with the Norman system. Initially, William had confiscated only the land of those nobles who had opposed him at Hastings. But various rebellions and the increasing demands of his barons had caused him to carry the process of confiscation to an extreme. By 1086, as the Domesday survey shows, there remained only two major Anglo-Saxon landowners—Thurkill of Arden and Colswein of Lincoln—and only about eight percent of the country was still under English lordship. The Church, too, had suffered: Only one of fourteen bishoprics was still in Saxon hands, and there were no more than three native abbots.

Thus the Norman Conquest had completely transformed English society by the extinction of the old aristocracy and the creation of a new and foreign ruling class. An English population of at least 1.5 million had been made subservient to a tiny minority of approximately 10,000 Normans, Frenchmen, and Flemings who had settled there since 1066.

The Domesday survey was completed in 1087. Very probably William never saw it. About that time he was leading a campaign in the Vexin, a territory disputed with the Frankish king. In July, the first Norman king of England, now sixty years old, rode at the head of his troops into the burning town of Mantes. Suddenly his horse stumbled on a smoldering ember, and William was thrown against the pommel of his saddle, sustaining injuries from which he died at Rouen some five or six weeks later. Before his death, he confirmed his unruly son Robert as heir to the duchy of Normandy; England he bequeathed to his second surviving son, William.

In terms of human suffering, the two decades of his reign had been disastrous for the English people, who had seen their lands taken from them and their ancient ways changed by foreign oppressors. In the long term, though, the Normans brought much

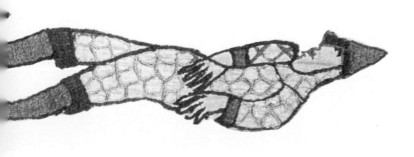

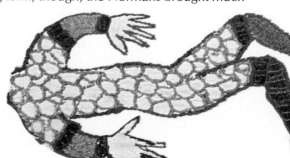

An Inventory of a Nation

The *Domesday Book,* an economic survey of Norman England, was undertaken by the order of King William about 1086. The book records in note form the findings of an army of commissioners sent throughout the country to determine patterns of land tenure. The basic unit of assessment was the manor, usually identical to an earlier Saxon village but at this time generally the property of a Norman lord. To determine the productive capacity of each manor, the investigators sought to determine how many plow teams it supported; they also were careful to list such other assets as watermills, woodland, and pasture.

The outlined entry, rendered into modern English on the right, comes from a list of the manors held by one of England's few female landowners, the countess Judith—a distant relative of the Conqueror—in the central county of Northamptonshire. In Willybrook Hundred—an administrative unit made up of several villages within the county—she was lord of the manor of Fotheringhay, where she held six hides of land—equivalent to about 750 acres. Only a third of her holding was in lordship—retained as demesne land for her own use and worked by serfs, or slaves. The rest of the manor was occupied by villagers who were nominally free though bound by feudal obligation to put in a given amount of work each week on the demesne.

TERRA SIGAR DE CIOCHES.

...GAR de Cioches ten de rege .iiii. his In Tovecestr hd ...parte dim hide. Tra e .x. car. De hac .i. hida ...dnio .iii. car. 7 v. serui. 7 iii. ancille. 7 xxi. uilli ...63 7 xi. bord hnt. uiii. car. Ibi. uiii. ac pa. Silua ...pe lg .iiii. q̃p lat. Valuit 7 ual. vi. lib. Tosti tenuit.

...RRA SVAIN. In Clavestou hd ...iiii. ten de rege .iiii. his in Stoche. Tra e .x. car. ...nio e. una. 7 xiiii. uilli cu pbr̃o 7 vii. bord hnt. v. car. ...molin de .xii. sol. 7 iii. den. 7 xxx. ac pa. Silua .iii. ...7 ii. q̃ dim lat. Valuit 7 ual. iii. lib.

...RRA SIBOLDI. In Hochesl hd ...bus ten de rege una 7 dim. 7 dim in Ludewic. Tra e ...7 dim. De hac tra e una v in dnio. Ibi .i. car. 7 ii. ...ii. bord. cu dim car. Valuit .iiii. sol. modo. x. sold. ...Lebe tenuit T.R.E.

...RRA OGERII. In Lapestou hd ...rus ten de rege .ii. his 7 dim in Lapestone. Tra e. v. ...n dnio fc .ii. car. cu .i. seruo. 7 vii. uilli 7 v. bord hnt. i. car. ...ochi cu .i. car. Ibi molin de .xx. sol. 7 xii. ac pa. Silua ...lg. 7 iiii. q̃d lat. Valuit 7 ual. iiii. lib.

...RRA DROGON DE BEVREIRE. In Winemeresle hd ...go de Beureire ten de rege .i. hid 7 iii. v. 7 tcia in Cedes ...Tra e. v. car. In dnio .e. i. car. cu .i. seruo. 7 x. uilli ...bord cu .iiii. car. Silua .i. q̃ lg 7 tcia lat. ...e. xx. sol. modo. xl. sol. Vlf tenuit ho Wulfef. ...a comitissa calumpni.

...RRA MANNONIS In Svtone hd. ...no ten de rege .i. hid in Taneford. Tra e .ii. car 7 dim. ...e una. 7 ii. serui. 7 ii. uilli hnt .i. car 7 dim. ...ire molin .xxx. den. Valuit 7 ual. xl. sold. Algar ...enuit. T.R.E. In Clavesle hd.

...ten .i. in Wiebe. Tra e. iii. car. In dnio fc. iii. ...uo. 7 vi. uilli cu .i. bord hnt .ii. car. Ibi .iii. ac. Silua ...tid lg. 7 iii. q̃ lat. Valuit 7 ual. xl. sol. Steinuart libe ...ten de. xi. iiii. his 7 iii. partes uni v In Fotala hd ...develle. Tra e. vii. car. In dnio una. cu .i. seruo. ...uilli 7 ii. sochi. modo. xl. sold. Laurus libe tenuit In Wenelle ...7 vi. sol. modo. xl. sold. Laurus libe tenuit ...7 pan una v tra in Bratone. h cu appendic.

...RRA EVSTACHII. ...tachius ten de rege .i. hid 7 ii. v tra 7 dim in Islham. ...i. car. In dnio e una. 7 vi. uilli 7 ii. bord cu .i. car. ...molin de .x. sol. 7 v. ac pa. Valuit 7 ual. xl. sold. ...tra occupauit ut Eustach sup ecclam de Ramesy. ...ul3 ten de. E. ii. his in Averstone. Tra e. v. car. ...e una. 7 viii. uilli 7 v. bord cu .ii. car 7 dim. Ibi molin ...den. 7 vii. ac pa. Silua .iii. q̃ lg 7 ii. q̃ lat. ...x. solid. modo. xxx. sold. Norman tenuit ho .ii. teign. ...3 ten de. E. in Pochebroc. i. his 7 una v tra. Tra e. ii. ...dnio. e. una. 7 iiii. uilli cu pbr̃o 7 vii. bord hnt cu .ii. car 7 dim. ...i. sol. modo. xx. sold. Ornar libe tenuit. ...u3 ten de. E. dim his in Winewincle. Tra e. ii. car. ...e una. cu .i. seruo. 7 iiii. uilli cu .i. car. Ibi .iii. ac pa. ...x. sol. modo. xl. sold. Achi tenuit. In Fevresleu hd ...u3 ten de. E. dim his in Walestone. Tra e. i. car. ...e cu .i. q̃ boif. Valuit 7 ual. v. sold. In Lapestou hd ...ten de. E. .i. his 7 una v tra in Dodine. Tra e. ii. car. ...e una. 7 ii. uilli cu .iiii. bord hnt dim car. Valuit .iii. sol. ...modo. x. sold.

TERRA IVDITE COMITISSE. In Wicelea Wapent.

IVDITA Comitissa ten de rege .i. his 7 dim in Riehale Botesl ...Tra. e. viii. car. cu appendic. In dnio. e. una. 7 iiii. serui. 7 x. ...uilli 7 ii. sochi hnt .iiii. car. Ibi .ii. molin de. xx 7 vi. solid. ...Silua .iiii. q̃ent lg. 7 ii. q̃ lat. ...Huic m̃ pan Belmestorp. Ibi .i. hida 7 dimid. 7 in dnio .ii. ...car. 7 xiii. uilli 7 vi. bord hnt .iiii. car. Ibi molin de. x. sol. ...7 viii. den. 7 xvii. ac pa. Tot ualuit 7 ual. vi. lib. ...Ipsa ten tcia parte uni hide in Ascet. Ibi ft .iii. sochi reddt ...p ann. v. sol. 7 iiii. den. ...In Svtone. e. dim hida 7 tcia pars dim hide. 7 ibi .iiii. sochi hnt ...i. car. 7 dim. 7 reddt p ann .x. sol 7 viii. den. ...In Westone. e. i. hida 7 tcia pars .i. hide. 7 ibi .v. sochi ...hnt .i. car 7 dim. 7 reddt p ann. xxi. sol. 7 i. den. ...In Tingleia. e. tcia pars uni hide. 7 iii. partes .iiii. partu ...uni hide. 7 ibi .v. sochi cu .i. car 7 dim 7 reddt vi. sol 7 vi. ...In Brantone. e. i. hida. 7 ibi .iiii. sochi hnt .ii. car. 7 Senar ...7 reddt p ann. v. sol. 7 vii. den.

Ipsa comit ten .vi. his in Foderingeia. In Wilebroc hd ...Tra e .xii. car. De hac tra .ii. hide ft in dnio 7 ibi .iii. car. ...7 iii. serui. 7 xix. uilli cu pbr̃o 7 vi. bord hnt. ix. car. Ibi ...molin de .viii. sol. 7 xl. ac pa. Silua .i. leu lg 7 ix. q̃ lat. ...cu oner̃ee 7 rex in ea n uenat. ual. x. solid. ...Valuit. viii. lib. modo. xii. lib. Turchil libe tenuit. T.R.E.

...psa. co. ten. ... In dnio fc. iiii. car. 7 una Ancilla. 7 xxvi. uilli 7 vi. ...bord 7 vi. sochi hnt .x. car. Ibi molin de. v. sol. 7 v. q̃ent ...pa in lg. 7 ii. q̃ lat. Silua .viii. q̃ lg. 7 i. leuul 7 iii. q̃ lat. ...Valuit 7 ual. x. lib. Turchil libe tenuit.

...In Lancesport. e. una bouata tre cu .i. bord. reddt. xvi. denar. ...In Bradeford. e. dim̃ 7 tcia v de soca. Ibi uni uilli ht dim car. ...Valuit 7 ual. iiii. sold.

...In Brestone ft .i. v tra 7 dim̃. Ibi .iii. sochi hnt .ii. car. ...Valuit 7 ual. x. solid.

...In Burtone. e. una hida 7 dim de soca. Tra. e. iii. car. h af ...hnt ibi .iiii. sochi cu .iiii. uilli 7 v. bord. 7 viii. ac pa.

...In Cranesleie. e. una hida. 7 ibi. vi. sochi cu v. bord hnt ...ii. car. 7 vi. ac pa.

...In Hanintone ft ... v tra 7 ibi .iiii. sochi hnt .i. car 7 dim. ...7 ii. ac pa. h e. iii. tre ual. xl. sol. m̃. xvi. denar plus.

...Ipsa. co. ten. iiii. his in Bartone. Tra e. viii. car. In dnio fc .ii. ...7 ii. serui. 7 viii. uilli 7 vi. bord 7 xi. sochi hnt. vi. car. Ibi .ii. ...molin de. xx. ual. sol 7 xii. den. 7 xviii. ac pa. Valuit 7 ual. ...iiii. lib. Bondi tenuit cu saca 7 soca.

...Ipsa. co. ten. iiii. his in Witbei. Tra e. vi. car. In dnio e. ...una. 7 vii. sochi hnt .vi. car. Valuit 7 ual. iiii. lib. Bondi tenuit.

...Ipsa. Co. ten. iiii. his in Aset. Tra. e. vi. car. In dnio. e. una. ...7 ii. serui. 7 vi. uilli 7 vi. bord cu. vii. sochi hnt. vi. car. ...Valuit 7 ual. iii. lib. Bundi tenuit. he. m̃. xii. pars in Bartone.

...In Brohestone ft. iii. v tre de soca. Tra. e. iii. car. 7 dimid. ...h af hnt ibi. iiii. sochi cu. iii. bord. In Winmaresle hd.

...Ipsa. co. ten. iii. his 7 dim in Gerdell. Tra. e. xi. car. De ...hac tra. e in dnio. i. hida. 7 ibi. iii. car. 7 xvi. uilli cu vii. bord ...hnt. vi. car.

In Willybrook Hundred: The Countess holds six hides herself in FOTHERINGHAY. Land for twelve plows. In lordship two hides of this land, three plows there; three slaves.

Nineteen villagers with a priest and six smallholders have nine plows.

A mill at eight shillings; meadow, forty acres; woodland, one league long and nine furlongs wide; value when stocked and the king is not hunting in it, ten shillings.

The value was eight; now twelve. Thorkell held it freely before 1066.

to the country. The English language was to be enriched through contact with the French spoken by the new, Norman aristocracy and the Latin of the clergy and bureaucrats. The king's men were great builders, too, and their constructions brought a new scale and assertiveness to English architecture. The White Tower, built in London in about 1078, set a style for similar stone keeps that commanded the surrounding lands, replacing the timber halls of the vanquished Saxon lords. Stone, too, was used for the many new or rebuilt monasteries of William's reign, as well as for the great cathedral of Durham, the masterwork of Norman Romanesque architecture begun in 1093 in the time of William II.

Above all, the coming of the Normans brought new unity and security to a land constantly open to the threat of regional rebellion and Viking invasion. The great earldoms, which had been virtually independent states within the State, were dissolved, and William ensured that he himself was the largest landowner within most shires. Furthermore, he greatly strengthened central authority by attaching military obligation to every secular grant of land. In return for their property, his tenants had to swear to support the king with a fixed number of knights, fully equipped and trained, and to pay specified dues and to attend royal courts and councils.

It was essentially the same feudal system that was already operating in Normandy; in England, however, William was able to go much further. By the Oath of Salisbury of 1086, all landowners—not merely tenants-in-chief but also their knightly subtenants—were required to swear allegiance to the king. Thus a vassal's loyalty to the king could override his fealty to his immediate lord. The power of the English monarchy was thereby vastly increased, and by way of this advanced form of feudalism, the country was to become the most united and potentially the strongest state in the world of Latin Christendom.

While England was coming to terms with its new overlords, other Normans were also carving out principalities for themselves far away on the other side of Europe. Decades before the Hastings campaign was even conceived, bands of knights, spurred by personal ambition and the hope of territory rather than by any grand design of their duke, had made their presence felt in the south of Italy, almost 1,000 miles away from their homeland. In the process, they played a crucial role in expanding the ever-widening gulf between the two divisions of Christendom: Latin and Greek, Rome and Constantinople.

At the beginning of the century, Italy was a fragmented country. To the north, the land lay under the suzerainty of the German emperors; in the center, the Papal States stretched from Rome to Ravenna. Southern Italy was meanwhile split between feuding Lombards—who ruled the autonomous principalities of Capua, Salerno, and Benevento—and Greeks, whose provinces of Apulia and Calabria (respectively the heel and toe of the Italian peninsula) formed part of the Byzantine Empire. Across the Strait of Messina, Sicily had been in Arab hands since the ninth century. These southern lands offered promising opportunities for military adventurers.

There would be conflicting accounts of how the Normans first came to be involved in the power struggles of southern Italy. The best-known account would date their involvement from about 1016, when forty Norman pilgrims, returning from the Holy Land, stopped over to visit the famous shrine of the Archangel Michael at Monte Gargano on the east coast. There they were approached by a Lombard noble named Melo who was planning a revolt to free Apulia from Byzantine rule. He wanted to recruit mercenaries for his cause, and he stressed that immense wealth was to be gained by those who fought to establish Lombard domination of the south.

Some of the pilgrims, it seems, promised to join him the following year; and certainly, from 1017 onwards, southern Italy was the destination of increasing numbers of Norman knights and adventurers in search of wealth and glory. Loyal only to themselves, they hired out their swords so haphazardly that sometimes Norman would meet Norman on the field of battle.

Typical of the opportunism of the time was the career of Rainulf, a Norman mercenary who distinguished himself in defending the duchy of Naples against a Lombard invasion by Prince Pandulf III of Capua. In 1030, Duke Sergius of Naples rewarded him with a fief of his own—the town and territory of Aversa. It must have seemed a sound tactical move to the duke, since Aversa, lying directly between Naples and Capua, could serve as a barrier to any fresh advance by the Lombard prince. Rainulf, however, simply used the fief to build up a personal power base. By way of marriage, he allied himself to his former enemy Pandulf III. Later, he changed sides yet again, and for his part in the overthrow of Pandulf was rewarded with the title of count.

Rainulf was the first Norman to secure a territorial foothold in Italy, but others soon followed his example. Foremost among them were three sons of a minor Norman knight called Tancred de Hauteville. The eldest, William, journeyed over the Alps to Italy in about the year 1035. At first he served with Rainulf, but later, at the head of several hundred Norman mercenaries, joined the Byzantine emperor in an attempt to recover Sicily from the Arabs. The campaign was a failure, but William gained great fame as a warrior; during a siege of the ancient city of Syracuse, he spotted the city's redoubtable military governor, whom he charged, unhorsed, and killed. For this feat he was given the sobriquet of Bras-de-Fer—Iron-arm. Back in Italy, he fought for the Lombards against the Greeks and, in 1042, was rewarded with the title of count of Apulia. So in seven years, he had advanced from obscurity to a position of nobility and military power. Remarkably, however, his progress was to be eclipsed by his two younger half brothers, Robert and Roger.

Robert de Hauteville rode into Capua in the autumn of 1046. He was an exceptionally striking figure—tall, broad shouldered, and flaxen haired, according to the Byzantine emperor's daughter, the historian Anna Comnena, who once met him—and at the age of thirty was thirsting for action and advancement. Getting no help from his fully engaged brother William, he struck out on his own, establishing a private band of freebooters in Calabria. There he pillaged the Byzantine countryside and outwitted all opposition to such effect that he became known throughout the province as Robert Guiscard, Robert the Cunning.

In the meantime, William Bras-de-Fer had died childless, and Apulia, along with the rest of southern Italy, was rent by warring factions. This state of strife so disturbed Pope Leo IX that he wrote to the Byzantine emperor Constantine IX to condemn the Normans who, he claimed, "with an impiety which exceeds that of the pagans, rise up against the Church of God, causing Christians to perish by new and hideous tortures, sparing neither women, children, nor the aged." The letter must have had some effect, for an alliance was formed in 1053. It was arranged that the papal and Byzantine forces should link up near Siponto in northern Apulia to take on the Norman scourge.

In fact, the pope's army never reached Siponto. On June 17, on a high plain in the

THE CONQUEROR'S STONE KEEP

In the closing decades of the eleventh century, the Normans completed the largest secular stone building to be constructed in Britain since Roman times: a riverside fortress that overawed the people of London and symbolized the permanence of the new regime. The White Tower—still the core of the present-day Tower of London—in its original form was a three-story, turreted structure standing almost ninety feet high. It was defended by massive walls and a moat that filled with the tidal overflow of the nearby Thames River.

An earlier wooden tower, built at the time of the Norman occupation of the city in 1066, stood in the forecourt, alongside stables, kitchens, and storage huts. To the south, a small gate gave access to the river, but the main entrance was via a timber bridge and a fortified entrance through the palisade atop its earthen west wall.

The keep itself could be entered only by external stairs leading to the first floor. It seemed impregnable. Nine centuries later, it still stands secure, dwarfing the smaller towers built around it in later centuries.

Apennines near the city of Civitate, it was met by a Norman force led by Robert Guiscard and Richard, count of Aversa. Faced with the prospect of being driven from Italy, the Normans, for the first and last time, had combined to present a united front. In so doing, these enthusiastic champions of the Church had shown that they were prepared, however reluctantly, to raise their standard even against the Vicar of Christ.

From the ramparts of his palace, Pope Leo witnessed the murderous onslaught of the Norman knights and the overwhelming defeat of his men. Fearing for his own life, he sought refuge in the nearby city of Benevento, but its citizens refused him asylum and handed him over to the victors. Meeting him in person, the Normans saw him no longer as their enemy, but rather as their spiritual leader; they fell to their knees, kissing his sandals and begging his forgiveness for their deeds. Nonetheless, while extending him the utmost courtesy, they continued to keep him confined in the city until, after nine months, he finally agreed to recognize their rule. Five weeks later, Leo died, a broken man.

Embroidered in gold thread on a red silk mantle, a stylized Tree of Life separates mirror-images of a lion mauling a camel. Made for Roger II, the second Norman count (and later first Norman king) of Sicily, the cloak is bordered with an Arabic inscription extolling the many virtues of its owner. Like his father before him, Roger was an enlightened ruler of a multiracial nation, under whose tolerant supervision the cultures of three great civilizations—Latin, Greek, and Arab—coexisted in relative harmony.

The battle of Civitate was a turning point for the Normans of southern Italy. Thereafter they were never again confronted by the prospect of a united opposition. They took advantage of the victory to extend their conquests, although consolidating these gains in the face of the hostility of the local people was to prove a sterner task.

Robert Guiscard was the leader most severely threatened. Already the master of much of Calabria, he inherited the title of count of Apulia in 1057 to become by far the most powerful landowner south of the Papal States. His military resources, however, were barely adequate to control the wild and mountainous lands under his authority, with their unreconciled, largely Greek-speaking inhabitants. When, faced with crippling taxation and the threat of famine, the whole of Norman Calabria rose in revolt in 1058, Robert needed help urgently and in desperation turned to his younger brother Roger.

Twenty-eight years of age, Roger was the last of the Hauteville brothers to settle in Italy, and he was also the most charismatic. An admiring biographer described him as "a handsome youth, tall and well-built. He was very ready of speech, but his gay and open manner was controlled by calculating prudence. Brave and valiant himself, he was fired by the ambitions proper to his years, and he sought by means of lavish gifts and favors to collect a party of adherents who would be devoted to furthering his fortunes." He succeeded so well that within only a year of his arrival he had raised an army strong enough to suppress the rebellion. In return for his services, however, he demanded that Robert Guiscard should cede to him half of the troublesome territory, as well as the remainder of Byzantine Calabria yet to be conquered.

By this time, the Normans had come to dominate almost all of southern Italy. In the west, Richard of Aversa had seized the principality of Capua, leaving only small areas under Lombard control; the only remaining Greek territories were a small portion of Calabria and the strongly fortified port of Bari, which was the headquarters for the Byzantine army in Italy.

Already in the ascendant, the Normans now received a fresh impetus to expansion from a completely unexpected quarter. In 1059, the new pope Nicholas II journeyed to southern Italy to thank the Normans for the assistance they had given to him in winning election to the papal throne. In the course of his visit, he confirmed Richard as prince of Capua and invested Robert Guiscard with the dukedoms of Apulia and Calabria. More unexpectedly, he also made the offer, which was gratefully accepted, of a third dukedom: Sicily, an island on which Robert had never set foot and over which the pope at the time had no authority. In return, the Normans swore an oath of allegiance to Nicholas and to the Church of Rome.

The reasoning underlying this unexpected alliance was clear enough. After the disaster of Civitate, Vatican diplomats had realized that Norman victories over the Orthodox Greeks, who owed their religious allegiance to the patriarch of Constantinople, could work to Rome's advantage. Furthermore, Pope Nicholas looked with great favor on Robert Guiscard's ambitions to conquer Sicily, thereby restoring Christian control over the island.

With the seal of papal approval to encourage his enterprise, Duke Robert set to work with a will. Campaigning with his brother Roger, he took Reggio, the capital of Byzantine Calabria, and Messina, along with most of northeast Sicily, within a few months of his investiture. Rebellion in the Greek territories then compelled him to return to mainland Italy, leaving his brother to continue the Sicilian campaign. His solution to the unrest was to seek to eradicate once and for all the Greek presence by destroying the apparently impregnable port of Bari. To this end, he isolated the Greek stronghold, encircling it with troops by land and with a barricade of boats chained together at sea.

For more than two years Bari held out, sustained by the hope of salvation in the form of a Byzantine relief force. Eventually one came; but it failed to penetrate the Norman sea defenses, and nine of the twenty Byzantine vessels were sunk. Their last hope gone, the inhabitants finally surrendered to Robert in April 1071. Later that year, the victor returned to Sicily, where he and his brother launched another combined operation on sea and land to take the capital, Palermo.

Even these heady triumphs could not exhaust the ambition of the Hauteville brothers. Having driven the Byzantines from Italy, Robert then aspired to the conquest of the Byzantine capital of Constantinople itself. In 1081, he crossed the Adriatic with an army, and at Durazzo, capital of the province of Illyria, defeated a Byzantine force commanded by the Greek emperor in person. Constantinople seemed to be within his grasp; but once more he had to return to Apulia to put down local rebellions fostered by Byzantine agents. In 1085, he resumed his eastern campaign, only to fall victim, at the age of seventy, to an epidemic of fever—probably typhoid—which decimated his army.

In the meantime, Robert's brother Roger was pressing on with the conquest of Sicily; at the moment of Robert's death he was besieging Syracuse. Within a few years, he succeeded in mopping up the last Islamic resistance and made himself undisputed master of the island. Unlike Robert, he favored wherever possible the path of negotiation, a policy of accommodation that he was to continue as count of Sicily. Recognizing the need for religious tolerance in a divided community, he acknowledged Arabic as an official language, left many Muslim governors at their posts, and allowed them to dispense Islamic justice from their courts. His wisdom and statesmanship won him widespread respect. By the time of his death in 1101, Roger was ranked among the greatest princes of Europe; the kings of France, Germany, and Hungary all sought dynastic alliances with his family. He has gone down in history as the Great Count, a warrior in the true Norman mold who nonetheless brought political stability and growing prosperity to a land of Latins, Greeks, and Muslims.

His example was the more striking in that his contemporaries in Europe were by then committed to the fiercely partisan adventure of the First Crusade. Normans were in the forefront of the crusading armies, and none played as prominent a part as another Hauteville: Count Bohemond, Robert Guiscard's eldest son. Inheriting his father's imposing stature and military prowess, Count Bohemond quickly established

The Normans had a genius for adapting existing techniques to suit their own purposes, and one age-old military tactic that they put to new use was that of siege mining. Used at least since classical times, the stratagem of digging under an enemy's fortifications acquired added relevance with the development of castle building in stone in the late eleventh century. In southern Italy and the Levant, Norman engineers sought to bring down the walls of places they were besieging by undermining them. Wooden pit props served for temporary support while the work was in progress; once all was ready, brushwood was used to fire them and bring the fortification tumbling down. To avoid alerting the defenders, the tunnel entrance was usually concealed behind rising ground or trees (inset).

himself as one of the leaders of the expedition; and when the city of Antioch fell to the crusaders in 1098 after a siege of seven months' duration, Bohemond was chosen to be its ruler. The independent principality thereby established was to survive for a period of 170 years.

So it came to pass that, over the course of the eleventh century, the Normans succeeded in creating a piecemeal empire, bound by family and ethnic ties rather than by a unified political command, that incorporated lands as diverse as Britain, the Mediterranean littoral, and the Levant. A single thread linked their various enterprises: military superiority. The Normans were without question the finest European soldiers of their day, and their triumphs would be among the greatest warrior success stories in all of history.

Any number of reasons would be suggested for the predominance of the Normans: their development of existing cavalry techniques; their skill in castle building and siege warfare; even the practice of primogeniture in a nation of large families, a custom that created a host of unpropertied younger sons ambitious for land and glory. But perhaps their greatest asset was a genius for adaptation and imitation. They were not innovators; almost everything in the Norman heritage, whether in architecture, religion, or even warfare, can be traced back to some other source, be it French or Italian or Anglo-Saxon. In truth, the Normans learned from almost everyone with whom they came into contact, modifying and systematizing what they found until it suited their own purposes.

In so doing, they sometimes radically changed the original, for example by superimposing over the confusion of tenth-century Europe the superstructure of centralized feudal states. They thereby provided, in William's England and in Roger's Sicily, good and firm government at a time when that commodity was rare. They proved themselves great conquerors and assured rulers; but because in cultural terms they took more from those they conquered than they brought with them, their ultimate fate was to change the character of Europe and then, as a separate people, to vanish from the face of the earth.

A RELIGIOUS POWERHOUSE

The Benedictine abbey at Cluny in eastern France was the largest and most magnificent of all the eleventh-century European monasteries. It was founded by William the Pious, Duke of Aquitaine, in 910, at a time when Europe was in a state of virtual anarchy and the Church was in serious moral decline, when priests could buy their parishes and even monks had wives. But the eleventh century was to see widespread reform, with Cluny in its vanguard. Under a series of brilliant and devout abbots, it rose in prestige to become one of the most powerful institutions in Christendom.

The monks of Cluny, many of whom were aristocrats, lived under a strict version of the monastic rule drawn up by Saint Benedict in the sixth century; most of the hours the saint had set aside for daily labor the Cluniac monks added instead to an already crowded devotional schedule of chants, masses, private prayers, and sacred readings. For the Cluniacs' duty was the perpetual praise of God and intercession for the sins of the world. The bulk of the work in their monasteries and farms was done by lay brothers, servants, and serfs.

The abbots of Cluny quickly acquired a

reputation for holiness that helped spread their influence around Europe. Rulers eager to reform existing houses or to found new ones would send to Cluny for monks to supervise the process. In this way, the mother house eventually created a few hundred dependencies. Unlike other monastic foundations, however, those of the Cluniac Order were not self-governing. All their monks owed their allegiance directly to the abbot of Cluny. He was the one who chose their priors; and to become full members of the order they had to travel to Cluny to make their vows before him.

Nor was Cluny's influence limited to the monasteries. It touched the administration of the Church, providing Rome with bishops, cardinals, and several popes. It even impinged on affairs of state because its abbots were the confidants of kings; critics of the abbots said these Cluniac holy men were like kings themselves.

At the Council of Rome in 1077, Pope Gregory VII declared that "among all the abbeys beyond the Alps, there shines first and foremost that of Cluny." He was understating the case; Cluny was without equal even in the land of the Holy See itself.

Duke William founded Cluny with only a farm and a simple chapel, but the endowments of later benefactors enabled each succeeding abbot to make the abbey larger and more splendid. The greatest of the builders was Hugh, abbot from 1049 to 1109, who was canonized eleven years after his death. During his stewardship, the number of monks rose from 60 to 300, and he expanded the domestic quarters to accommodate them. But his most important construction was Cluny's church—the third since the original foundation—which he began in 1088. Until the rebuilding of Saint Peter's in Rome, completed in 1612, it was the largest church in the world.

As the plan at left shows, Saint Hugh's new refectory stood beyond the cloister on the left of the church, with the chapter house and dormitory in front of it. Other buildings included workshops, kitchens, stables, guest quarters, an infirmary, and a hospice for travelers.

1 REFECTORY

2 DORMITORY

3 CHAPTER HOUSE

4 CHURCH

SPACE FOR SLEEPING

All the monks at Cluny, including the abbot, slept on straw mattresses in one dormitory above the chapter house. The abbot's mattress was in the middle. In Saint Hugh's day, the room was about 165 feet long and had ninety-seven windows, each as tall as a man with his arms stretched upward, so that the monks had enough light to read by during rest periods. Beyond the dormitory there was a washroom and dozens of latrines, each one with a little window above it.

The fullest account of daily life at Cluny was written by a monk called Ulrich around 1083. At about 2:30 in the morning, the monks rose at the sound of a bell, dressed by the light of three lamps, which were kept burning throughout the night, and went down to the church to sing nocturns. This was the earliest of a series of offices known as the regular hours, which punctuated their entire day. After that they returned briefly to bed before rising again for vigils and then matins at dawn.

Before matins they washed their hands and faces and combed their tonsured hair in the cloister. Every Tuesday they put their dirty clothes in a chest; the launderers returned the clothes on the following Saturday. But the monks only shaved once a week. "As for our baths," wrote Ulrich, "there is not much that we can say, for we only bathe twice a year, before Christmas and before Easter."

MEETING PLACE FOR MONKS

The daily assembly known as the chapter took place in the chapter house after the first morning mass. It began with prayers and the reading of a chapter from the Benedictine Rule, which gave the assembly its name. After that the abbot proceeded to the business of the day, which included such worldly responsibilities as administering abbey property and keeping the buildings in good repair. Although the monks were entitled to express opinions on most matters, it was the abbot who made all the decisions, and his inferiors were not allowed to argue with him or discuss issues with one another.

Another duty of the chapter was the disciplining of offenders. If a monk had committed a small, or venial, sin, he was beaten with a rod and then barred from eating with his brothers and made to prostrate himself before the altar during services until the abbot absolved him. If his sin was more serious, such as drunkenness, blasphemy, or talking to women, he was not even allowed to enter the church. After he had been absolved, this wrongdoer was beaten again, and for a while he had to undertake the most humble duties before being fully reinstated. When that happened, however, his colleagues had to bow before him in order to avoid the sin of pride at not having transgressed themselves.

CORE OF THE COMMUNITY

Saint Hugh's enormous Romanesque church measured 460 feet from door to apse. The walls were decorated with paintings. The building had five aisles, two transepts and almost 500 sculptured column-capitals, and the arches in the nave were among the first in the West to be pointed, in the Gothic manner, rather than round.

The story of the church's creation was as unusual as the splendor of its appointments. It was said to have been designed by saints and paid for by kings. Although the benefactors ranged from the poorest in the parish to the richest in all of Christendom, the largest donations came from Kings Alfonso VI of Castile and Henry I of England. And according to one chronicle, Saints Peter, Paul, and Stephen had revealed the design in a dream to a retired abbot called Gunzo who lived at Cluny.

The monks spent much more time in the church than anywhere else. After matins, the regular hours continued with prime, terce, sext around noon, nones, vespers at sunset, and compline about an hour later. Between these there were additional offices, particularly on feast days; and there were two morning masses, for which the monks remained standing throughout. The first was between prime and the chapter, and the second, the solemn mass, was usually after terce.

SETTING FOR SILENT MEALS

The refectory was another of the many buildings that Saint Hugh rebuilt to accommodate the growing number of monks. The monks usually met there twice a day, for dinner after sext at midday and for supper after sunset, between vespers and compline; during Lent, they ate only supper. After washing their hands, they took their places at one of the six tables in the body of the hall and remained standing until the abbot had taken his place at the high table.

The meal was eaten in silence while a brother read from the scriptures. The rule of silence forbade monks to speak at all on Sundays. During the week they were allowed to speak to one another only for brief periods after the chapter and between sext and dinner. But they developed an elaborate sign language that they used to communicate at other times, including gestures for verbs, objects, people, and every kind of food. An egg, for example, was signified by tapping one finger on another as if breaking a shell.

The Benedictine Rule forbade red meat. Dinner consisted of cooked dried beans, followed by cheese, or else eggs or fish, which were prepared by servants, and then fresh vegetables, which were cooked by monks. These foods together with bread, milk, honey, and a cup of wine each day, made up the bulk of the diet. All these items could be provided by Cluny's own farms, fishponds, and vineyards, but some food, particularly fish, came from benefactors as well. Count Eustace of Boulogne donated 20,000 pickled herring a year.

THE BIRTH OF RUSSIA

In the autumn of 989, Princess Anna, sister of the Byzantine emperor Basil II, began the voyage from Constantinople to the Crimea for her marriage to Grand Prince Vladimir of Kiev. Though brought up to show the virtues of obedience and humility, the princess was unable to contain her tears. "It is as if I were setting out into captivity," she is reported to have told her brother. "Better were it for me to die at home." Her anguish was hardly surprising, since stories about the "barbarians of the north" had long been circulating. Rumor had it that they worshiped hideous wooden idols, that they engaged in obscene rituals, even that they carried out human sacrifices. As for Vladimir himself, he was reputed to be insatiable in vice, with seven wives and 800 concubines. It was true that, as part of the bargain between himself and the emperor, the pagan prince had agreed to be baptized, but a young Christian princess might have been forgiven for suspecting that a man with his reputation was still a long way from salvation.

Yet in reality, Vladimir had embraced the new faith with an evangelical zeal that would not only lead to his eventual canonization but would transform the land he ruled—the kernel of the future Russian nation. His decision would turn his people toward Europe, rather than to the Islamic Middle East; yet by choosing the Orthodox faith of Constantinople rather than the Catholic communion of Rome, he ensured that a divide would remain between this eastern bastion of the Church and its western counterparts, among them the neighboring power of Poland, whose king had opted for Rome at the time of his conversion just twenty-two years earlier.

Vladimir's momentous resolve marked the culmination of a process of nation building stretching back over 120 years; and it gave birth to an extraordinary period in which his country would be more open to the outside world than its great offspring was to be for centuries to come. His principality of Kiev was to be the first state that could accurately be called Russian. It also produced the first Russian dynasty and saw Russia's rise for the first time into the ranks of the major powers.

The earlier history of the lands that would become Russia had been shrouded in darkness and violence. When, around AD 500, the forerunners of the Russians, the East Slavs, began pushing into the vast forest wilderness to the north and east of the Carpathian Mountains, they met with resistance from the Finnish and Lithuanian tribes who were already there. Thanks to the Slavs' superior weapons, however, they gradually absorbed or drove out the indigenous forest peoples.

To the south of the forest, in the immense, treeless steppe lands stretching from the Black Sea as far as the Great Wall of China, the Slavs were less successful. The steppe's flatness and its abundance of grazing made it a highway for the hordes of nomadic horsemen who regularly swept into Europe from central and eastern Asia. The first of these warlike peoples to burst upon the steppe had been the Scythians,

A detail from an eleventh-century mosaic in the Cathedral of Saint Sophia in Kiev shows the haloed head of the Virgin of the Annunciation. Built in 1037 and decorated mainly by imported Byzantine artisans, the church was one of many erected to embellish the Russian capital following the conversion of its ruler, the grand prince Vladimir, to Christianity in 988.

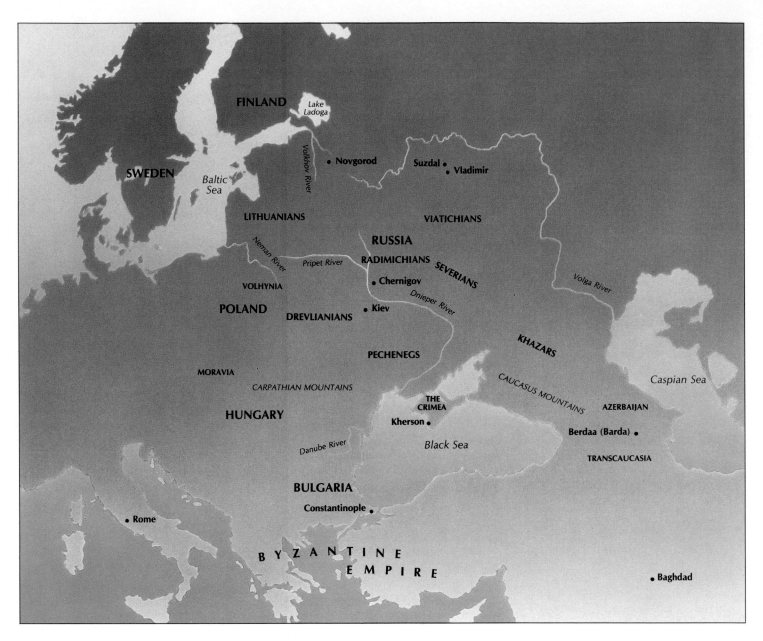

as early as 700 BC. They had been followed, in turn, by the Sarmatians, the Huns, the Avars, and the Khazars.

The Khazars, who arrived in the first half of the seventh century and remained until the start of the tenth, were more enlightened than their predecessors. Preferring to trade and farm rather than plunder and burn, they adopted a fairly tolerant attitude towards the Slavs. Some Slavs were even allowed to cultivate parts of the steppe, although they had to pay a high tribute for the privilege. Others moved to the wooded steppe, where patches of open grassland, alternating with islands of oak and birch, marked the frontier between the forest and the plain.

However, it was amid the perpetual gloom of the great forest itself, with its harsh climate, poor soil, and innumerable bogs, that the vast majority of the East Slavs came to settle. Here, before any crops could be planted, the peasants had first to carve out a clearing, felling the trees, then burning the stumps and undergrowth to produce fertilizer. After only three or four years of cultivation, the land was exhausted, at which point the whole process had to be repeated elsewhere in the forest.

This slash-and-burn method of farming could be practiced by small family units, and the Slavs organized themselves accordingly. Though divided into tribes and clans, their basic social grouping consisted of a handful of related households headed by a patriarch, usually the oldest male, who assigned the various tasks and made the important decisions. Property, including land, was held in common.

As a protection against the numbing cold, the Slavs built two types of dwellings. One was a simple log cabin with an insulating coat of clay; the other was a timber-lined dugout, sunk about twenty inches into the ground, then mounded over with earth for insulation. Though described by the sixth-century Byzantine historian Procopius as "wretched hovels," such dwellings would seem to have served their occupants well enough. Heating was provided by stoves made of stones or baked clay. However, since chimneys were unknown and smoke had to escape from under the eaves, the cold may sometimes have seemed preferable to the haze inside.

Travel was difficult in the dense forest, so most of the Slavic settlements were built on the banks of rivers, such as the Volkhov and the Dnieper, which served as ready-made transport routes. The size of settlements varied, but the larger ones would probably have included huts for storing and grinding grain, for weaving and sewing, and for smelting the iron deposits obtained from local bogs.

A constant danger for the early settlers, besides wolves and bears, was attack by rival tribes. In the forest, these were likely to be marauding groups of Finns and Lithuanians; on the steppe, freebooting bands of nomads looking for slaves and slaughter. Thus many settlements were fortified, usually with high wooden stockades, sometimes with ditches and earthen ramparts.

In such an environment, where the main concern was the most basic struggle for survival, there was little scope for social niceties. The *Primary Chronicle*, a twelfth-century account of Russia's earliest years as perceived from a Christian viewpoint, gives a vivid description of some of the more primitive pagan Slavic tribes: "The Drevlianians . . . existed in bestial fashion and lived like cattle. They killed one another, ate every impure thing, and there was no marriage between them, but instead they seized upon maidens by capture. The Radimichians, the Viatichians, and the Severians had the same customs. They lived in the forest like any wild beast and ate every unclean thing."

For all its perils and discomforts, the homeland of the East Slavs possessed two substantial assets: a seemingly endless supply of valuable forest products—furs, hides, amber from the Baltic region, honey, beeswax—and a superb system of interlocking waterways that enabled Slavic traders to ship such products to the distant markets of Khazaria and Byzantium. Here the Slavs were able to exchange their goods for luxury items, such as silks, wines, weapons, and ornaments. However, the Slavs were not the only people with an interest in the area. As early as the eighth century, small bands of Swedish Vikings, or Varangians as they were known, began probing along the waterways that led southward from the Baltic Sea and Lake Ladoga. Like their Danish and Norwegian compatriots, who were soon to descend upon the

The Kievan state—the first precursor of modern Russia—grew up along the river system linking the Baltic with the Black Sea. Swedish Vikings, known as Varangians, used the network of waterways linking Lake Ladoga to the Dnieper River to trade with the Byzantine Empire and its glittering capital, Constantinople. Along "the road from the Varangians to the Greeks," as it became known, the Varangians established riverbank trading posts from which they first conquered, and then assimilated with, the indigenous East Slavs. The state that developed from the mixing of the two races had its first capital at Novgorod, later supplanted by Kiev.

Following the Kievan ruler's adoption of Christianity, statues of the principal pagan deity Perun *(above)* were torn down and destroyed, and the human sacrifice associated with his worship was banned. But other elements of the old religion were incorporated into the new faith: Painted clay eggs associated with the Christian festival of Easter, such as the eleventh-century example opposite, derived from pagan models symbolizing springtime and fertility.

coasts of western Europe, the Varangians' overriding interest was in obtaining wealth—by trade or by the sword, as occasion demanded.

At first, they followed the network of rivers and portages that led to the Volga River and the Caspian Sea. Here they developed an extensive commerce with the Khazars and even journeyed onward to Baghdad. At this time, the Volga route lay outside the territories colonized by the Slavs, so the newcomers from Scandinavia left the Slavic population alone. However, early in the ninth century, attracted by the fabled riches of Byzantium, the Varangians began to thrust down the Volkhov and Dnieper rivers to the Black Sea—a route that took them through the heartland of the East Slavs.

As the Vikings proceeded southward, along what was to become famous as "the road from the Varangians to the Greeks," they clamped an iron grip upon the Slavic riverbank territories, either taking over existing settlements or founding new ones of their own. In some places the Slavs tried to resist, but they stood little chance against the veteran warriors from the far north, who fought with slashing, two-edged swords and murderous battle-axes.

Having established his domain, a Varangian chieftain would·exact as tribute from the local population a portion of the merchandise intended for export to the south. Part of this he would keep for his immediate needs—in particular, the payment of troops and retainers—and part he would send downriver under his own colors. As well as the usual forest products, such shipments also included captured opponents, bound for the slave markets of Constantinople. So regular was the supply of these prisoners that a special square in the Byzantine capital was set aside for their sale.

Despite the fact that, by the 820s, the Varangians had brought under their control the major section of the Baltic-Black Sea waterway, from Novgorod to Kiev, there was no single Varangian authority. Each ruler acted independently of the others, pursuing his own private interests and jealously guarding his own parcel of territory. According to tradition, it was in 862, with the so-called summoning of the princes, that the foundations of the first Russian state were laid. The only description of the event is in the *Primary Chronicle,* and since this document was intended to be as much a celebration of the ruling dynasty of the time as a historical record, it needs to be regarded with some reserve.

According to the *Chronicle,* in the middle of the ninth century the Slavs of the north grew tired of domination by the Varangians and succeeded in driving them out, but then fell into such discord among themselves that they asked the Varangians to return: "Our land is great and rich, but there is no order in it. Come to rule and reign over us." The call was answered by three brothers, of whom the eldest, Rurik, established himself in Novgorod. The chronicler refers to the Varangians led by Rurik as "Rusi" and describes the district of Novgorod as "the land of Rus." In later centuries, the phrase was to be latinized into Russia, an appellation that was gradually extended to the whole country.

A further decisive step was taken in 882, when Rurik's successor, Oleg, seized control of Kiev from a rival group of Varangians and brought, for the first time, the two most important towns of the north-south waterway under the sway of a single ruler. Oleg marked the event by proclaiming himself grand prince of Kiev, which became the capital of the enlarged Rus domain. Here, he was able to supervise, in person, the annual expedition to Byzantium that guaranteed his realm's prosperity.

Strategically located on the wooded steppe, just below the confluence of several smaller rivers with the Dnieper, Kiev served both as a collection point and as a dispatch center. Every spring, as soon as the ice on the waterways melted, scores of *monoxyles*—wooden boats, each built up from a scooped-out tree trunk—were floated down to the city from the upper reaches of the Dnieper, there to be loaded up with the tribute that the grand prince and his retainers had been collecting throughout the winter. The boats were then assembled into a great flotilla for the dangerous six-week journey through the open steppe to the Black Sea.

The most hazardous part of the route was a series of rock-strewn rapids starting about twenty-five miles south of Kiev. The Rus merchants managed to steer their way through the first three of the cataracts, but upon reaching the fourth they had to unload the boats and convey both these and the cargoes—slaves as well as goods—on foot, setting guards to protect themselves against the risk of ambush by the Pecheneg tribesmen of the region. After dragging or carrying the vessels overland for more than five miles, they could launch them once more on the river and reembark.

For the rulers of Kiev, Byzantium was more than their chief trading partner; it was also a prime source of plunder, and the two powers constantly alternated between uneasy alliance and open warfare. As early as 860, Oleg's Varangian predecessors in Kiev had launched a large-scale raid against Constantinople. In 907, setting forth allegedly with a fleet of 2,000 boats, Oleg mounted his own attack on the imperial city. Finding the harbor blocked by enormous chains, Oleg disembarked his men on the city's outskirts—where according to the chronicler they "accomplished much slaughter of the Greeks"—and put wheels on his boats to circumvent the barrier by transporting them overland, a stratagem that persuaded the worried Byzantines to sue for peace. By the terms of the settlement, Oleg extracted a huge indemnity and also forced the then coemperors Leo and Alexander to sign a trade treaty under which they

were obliged to pay for the food, accommodation, and provisioning of every Russian merchant who came to Constantinople. In return, the Russians undertook to enter the city through only one gate, not to appear in groups of more than fifty, and not to carry arms.

Oleg died in 913, having reportedly stepped on a venomous snake, and was succeeded by a fellow prince named Igor, who proved himself no less devoted to self-aggrandizement. He campaigned against not only the Christians of Byzantium—from whom he secured another favorable trade treaty—but also the Muslims of Transcaucasia to the southeast. The tenth-century Arab chronicler ibn Miskawaih wrote that in the years 943-944, "the army of the nation called the Rusi invaded Azerbaijan, where they attacked and seized Berdaa, taking its inhabitants captive. They know not defeat, nor does any of them turn back till he slay or be slain."

In fact, after several months spent plundering the country around Berdaa, the invading army was overwhelmed by superior Muslim forces, and their commander was killed. Igor, who had already returned to Kiev, did not long survive his general. He tried to extort double tribute from the Drevlianian tribes of the Pripet Basin, to the northwest of the city, provoking them into such fury that they murdered him. "If a wolf come among the sheep," the Drevlianian chief is reported to have told his followers, "he will take away the whole flock one by one, unless he be killed."

Although, by the time of Igor's death, the Kievan realm had established itself as a formidable military power, it was still made up of two distinct peoples: the ruling

Kiev's Byzantine Heritage

Although the Byzantine Empire was to suffer great disasters in the course of the eleventh century, during which it lost land on both its eastern and western borders, it remained one of the world's great centers of culture and civilization. The splendor of its churches and religious art, evinced here in a gilded and enameled silver icon of Archangel Michael, was a factor in Grand Prince Vladimir's choice of the Greek Orthodox faith rather than Roman Christianity or even Islam.

Byzantine artworks were widely imported into the Kievan state in the course of the eleventh century, and in the wake of the objects themselves came the artisans who made them. The styles they set for such artifacts as icons, mosaics, and jewelry pervaded Russian taste and provided the basis from which much of the nation's own decorative culture developed.

Nor was the Byzantine influence limited to the visual arts. Learning was disseminated through books written in the Cyrillic alphabet, devised in the ninth century by the Greek missionary Saint Cyril as a vehicle for the Slav tongue. Other works introduced the principles of Byzantine law, which influenced the first Russian legal code, promulgated in the mid-eleventh-century reign of Yaroslav the Wise.

Varangian minority and the subjugated Slavic majority. In every important sphere—political, diplomatic, commercial—the Varangians dominated. For example, in the treaty concluded in 945 between Igor and the Byzantines, all the signatories on the Kievan side bore Varangian names—Leif, Isgaut, Oleif, Sigbjorn, Freystein.

Yet it was to take less than a generation for the Varangian influence to disappear almost without trace. One of the factors promoting assimilation was the recruitment of Slavic warriors to replace Varangian members of the *druzhina*, or royal retinue, who had fallen in battle. Another, and perhaps more important, factor was intermarriage between Varangian men and Slavic women. Indeed, Igor's own wife, Olga, was a Slav, and their son, Sviatoslav, was the first prince of Kiev to be given a Slavic name.

Sviatoslav was still only a child when his father died, and it was Princess Olga who assumed power as regent. A woman of tough and determined character, she proved to be one of the most outstanding of the Kievan rulers. She made it her first priority to settle accounts with those who had killed her husband. When, according to the chronicler, a party of twenty Drevlianian envoys arrived in Kiev to propose a wedding match between Olga and their chief, the vengeful widow had them buried alive. She then inveigled the Drevlianians into sending a second party—"the best men who governed the land of Drevliania"—and these she had burned alive. Finally, she conquered and destroyed the main Drevlianian city of Iskorosten, killing many of its more venerable citizens and handing over others as slaves to her followers.

On a more positive note, Olga abolished the haphazard and arbitrary system of tribute by which the Varangians had exploited certain Slavic tribes and replaced it with taxes on the whole population. She also regulated the annual tribute-gathering expeditions of the grand prince, appointing local tax collectors to act on his behalf.

Of much greater consequence was Olga's encouragement of Christianity. She herself was baptized in 957, and from then until her death in 969, she strove for the conversion of her people. Olga was by no means the first of her race to embrace Christianity. Contacts with Byzantium and Bulgaria, converted in 864, had already led some Kievan merchants to adopt the new faith, and the chronicler mentions both Christians and pagans as endorsing the Kievan-Byzantine treaty of 945. Even so, in spite of this promising start, it was to take another quarter of a century for Christianity in Russia to develop the firm roots that Olga had hoped to encourage.

The opposition to the new faith centered around Olga's son, the young prince Sviatoslav, who feared that a surrender to Christianity would also be a surrender to one or other of the two Christian emperors—Roman or Byzantine. Indeed, Sviatoslav's intention was not merely to preserve his power but to increase it, and the whole of his short reign, from 962 to 971, was taken up with campaigns of conquest against neighboring states.

Moving, as the chronicler describes it, with the swiftness of a leopard, the grand prince paid scant regard to personal comfort. "Upon his expeditions he carried with him neither wagons nor kettles, and boiled no meat, but cut off small strips of horseflesh, game, or beef, and ate it after roasting it on the coals. Nor did he have a tent, but he spread out a horse blanket under him and set his saddle under his head; and all his retinue did likewise."

The result of such exertions was a string of conquests stretching from the Volga to the Danube. Even the ancient empire of the Khazars fell before the onslaught of Sviatoslav's marauders. However, each new Russian success aroused fresh apprehensions in Constantinople, and finally, in July 971, an army led by the Byzantine emperor John Tzimisces put paid to Sviatoslav's dream of imperial glory. With his own forces defeated, Sviatoslav was compelled to sign a humiliating peace treaty requiring him to give up all the territories that he had won. The signing of the treaty was followed by a personal meeting between Sviatoslav and Tzimisces on the Danube. An eyewitness at this meeting, the Byzantine historian Leo Diaconus, would provide a striking portrait of the grand prince: "The emperor arrived at the bank of the Danube on horseback, wearing golden armor, accompanied by a large retinue of horsemen in brilliant attire. Sviatoslav crossed the river in a kind of Scythian boat; he handled the oar in the same way as his men. His appearance was as follows: He was of medium height—neither too tall nor too short. He had bushy brows, blue eyes, and was snub nosed; he shaved his beard but wore a long and bushy mustache. His head was shaven except for a lock of hair on one side as a sign of the nobility of his clan. His neck was thick, his shoulders broad, and his whole stature pretty fine. He seemed gloomy and savage. On one of his ears hung a golden earring adorned with two pearls and a ruby set between them. His white garments were not distinguishable from those of his men except for cleanness."

Sviatoslav's first meeting with the Byzantine emperor also was his last. In destroying the power of the Khazars, Sviatoslav had opened the southern steppe to another host of belligerent Asiatic nomads, the Pechenegs, and it was a party of these who ambushed and killed him on his homeward journey past the Kiev cataracts. The Pechenegs, the chronicler says, overlaid his skull with gold and used it as a cup.

On the news of Sviatoslav's death, his three sons, Yarapolk, Oleg, and Vladimir, plunged into a bloody war of succession. Within a few months, Oleg was dead, Vladimir was in exile in Scandinavia, and Yarapolk was installed in Kiev as the grand prince. However, in 977, Vladimir returned to Russia with a war party of Varangian mercenaries, and a year later Kiev fell before his attack. Yarapolk was then murdered by the Varangians, which left Vladimir as the new ruler of Russia.

Possessed of the same dynamic energy that had spurred his father, Vladimir set about consolidating and strengthening his hard-won domain. In the forest steppe to the south, he built a ring of towns and fortifications to prevent further incursions by the Pechenegs; to the west, he recaptured territories that had been seized by the Poles during his war of succession; in the east, he brought to heel the Viatichians and the Radimichians, two of the tribes that had rebelled in the wake of Sviatoslav's death; and in the north, he conquered the Lithuanians and seized control of the Neman riverway to the Baltic.

At the same time, he encouraged a resurgence of paganism, crowning the hill near his castle with the idols of heathen deities. According to the chronicler, "The people sacrificed to them, calling them gods, and brought their sons and daughters to sacrifice them to these devils. They desecrated the earth with their offerings, and the land of Rus and this hill was defiled with blood."

Although the chronicler may well have exaggerated the amount of sacrificial bloodshed, there is no doubt about Vladimir's militant paganism. The reason for it would remain obscure. In the absence of his father as a result of constant campaigns, Vladimir must have grown up under the influence of his grandmother, Olga—a woman who would scarcely have refrained from teaching the Christian virtues to her grandson. On the other hand, Vladimir's brother Yarapolk had shown sympathy for the Christian party during the time of his brief rule in Kiev, and this may have prompted Vladimir to go to the other extreme. It is also possible that the multiplicity

Traders such as this one were among the main beneficiaries of Kiev's prosperity in the eleventh century. Departing each spring for Constantinople, they traveled down the Dnieper River with cargoes of furs, slaves, grain, honey, wax, and salt, to return with such Byzantine luxuries as silks, spices, and enamels. Their dress revealed the exotic influences they encountered on their travels, notably in the baggy, oriental-style trousers that were their trademark, while their swords testified to the hazardous nature of the journeys.

of idols reflected the tribal nature of paganism; Vladimir may have been trying to broaden his political support by showing respect to many different tribal gods.

In any event, in 988, some ten years after gaining the crown, Vladimir took the fateful step that was to lead both him and his country into the world of Christendom. According to the picturesque account given by the chronicler, Vladimir was approached, in 986, by representatives of various faiths who attempted to convert him. From a neighboring people, the Volga Bulgars, came a delegation preaching the attractions of Islam. In the next world, they promised, "Muhammad will give each man seventy fair women." This was a prospect that aroused Vladimir's interest, but when his visitors went on to explain that abstinence from wine was a principle of their faith, he promptly dismissed them. "Drinking," he said, "is the joy of the Rus. We cannot exist without that pleasure."

From another neighboring people, the Khazars, came a mission urging him to accept Judaism. (The ethnically non-Semitic Khazars had themselves been converted to Judaism around 865.) Asked by Vladimir where the Jews' native land was, they replied that "God was angry at our forefathers and scattered us among the gentiles on account of our sins. Our land was given to the Christians." Vladimir, who could see no merit in the faith of a dispersed people, dismissed the Khazars. A party of German emissaries from the pope fared little better. When they explained that their faith demanded prolonged fasting, Vladimir told them, "Depart hence; our fathers accepted no such principle."

The only case that did impress the grand prince was that put forward by the single representative from Byzantium—a Greek philosopher of some learning and much eloquence. Having presented a summary of both the Old and New Testaments, he held up an icon showing the Last Judgment, with the righteous, on the right, going to paradise, and the sinners, on the left, going to purgatory. If the grand prince wished to take his place upon the right, urged the philosopher, then he must be baptized.

Although Vladimir showered his guest with gifts and honors, he was still not entirely decided about which faith to adopt. He therefore dispatched a commission of ten "good and wise" men to observe the rites of each religion at first hand. Those of the Muslim Bulgars they found to be without glory; and those of the Jewish Khazars they ignored altogether. They were overwhelmed, however, by what they witnessed inside the Church of Saint Sophia, in Constantinople. "We knew not whether we were in heaven or on earth. For on earth there is no such splendor or such beauty, and we are at a loss how to describe it. We only knew that God dwells there among men, and their service is fairer than the ceremonies of other nations."

Thus, Vladimir is said to have found his way to the Eastern Orthodox faith. Whatever the account's truth, it is highly unlikely that Vladimir's conversion from paganism to Christianity was prompted by spiritual considerations alone. No doubt he also had in mind the fact that other European monarchs were Christian,

125

the king of Poland being only the most recent example, and that, in order to win their full approval and respect, he needed to follow their example. The event that brought matters to a head and ensured that Vladimir cast in his lot with Byzantium rather than Rome was a well-timed intervention by the Byzantine emperor Basil II.

Faced, in 987, with a rebellion that threatened to sweep him from power, the emperor appealed to Vladimir for military assistance. This Vladimir agreed to provide, but he demanded a high price in return—the hand of the emperor's sister, Princess Anna. No other Western ruler, not even a Christian, had been granted the honor of marrying into the imperial family, and Basil must have found it hard to swallow such impertinence from the Russian "barbarian." However, the threat to his throne outweighed the hurt to his pride, and early in 988, the bargain was struck.

The only condition was that Vladimir had to agree to accept Christianity for himself and his people. Accordingly, he was baptized in February 988, adopting the Christian name of Basil in honor of his future brother-in-law. Meanwhile, a corps of 6,000 Varangians set off from Kiev to Constantinople, arriving in time to swing the military balance in favor of the emperor. However, with the danger past, Basil became increasingly reluctant to send Anna to Russia. It was not, indeed, until Vladimir had captured the Byzantine city of Kherson, in the Crimea, and threatened Constantinople with a similar fate, that the emperor finally sent his anguished and weeping sister on her journey across the Black Sea.

The marriage ceremony was held in Kherson, after which Vladimir handed the city back to the emperor as *veno*—the bridegroom's gift. Vladimir and the grand princess then traveled on to Kiev, accompanied by a large number of ecclesiastics from the Crimea, who were to help him in his task of converting the Russian people.

Although the motives for Vladimir's own conversion may have been predominantly political, he plunged into his new faith with undeniable fervor. To the Russian Church of later years, he was to appear as a saint equal to the apostles in importance. Eulogizing him in the mid-eleventh century, the Kievan metropolitan Hilarion declared that it was through Vladimir's efforts that the Church in Russia had become "a wonder to all surrounding lands."

Vladimir's first act, on arriving back in Kiev, was to order the destruction of the pagan idols, a ceremony conducted with some drama. The statue of the Slavic thunder god, Perun, with its silver head and gold mustache, was bound to a horse and dragged to the Dnieper, there to be beaten with sticks and cast into the water. The following day, according to the chronicler, the whole population of Kiev, rich and poor alike, was instructed to go to the river to be baptized. Vladimir's lieutenants issued similar instructions to the inhabitants of Novgorod and the other cities.

As the old pagan sanctuaries were pulled down, new Christian churches sprang up in their place. These included the Kievan Church of the Dormition of the Holy Virgin (the Orthodox name for the Feast of the Assumption, celebrating Mary's ascent into heaven). Completed in 996, it was the first stone building of its kind in Russia. Vladimir brought in artisans from Greece to embellish it with frescoes and mosaics, and for its upkeep he assigned one-tenth of all his revenues, winning for the edifice the alternative title of the Church of the Tithe. However, it was through the example of his own life that Vladimir was to be chiefly remembered. As the chronicler portrays him, Vladimir not only preached the new faith but tried to put it into practice.

"He invited each beggar and poor man to come to the prince's palace and receive whatever he needed, both food and drink, and money from the treasury. With the thought that the weak and the sick could not easily reach his palace, he arranged that wagons should be brought in, and after having them loaded with bread, meat, fish, various fruits, mead in casks, and kvass, he ordered them driven out through the city. The drivers were under instructions to call out, 'Where is there a poor man or a beggar who cannot walk?' To such they distributed according to their necessities."

Less successful was Vladimir's attempt to apply Christ's injunction, "Resist not him that is evil," which he took to mean that criminals should not be punished. The result was that the countryside became overrun with bandits, and the clergy felt compelled to point out to him that to bring such malefactors to justice, far from being a sin, was one of the prime duties of a Christian prince. Reluctantly, Vladimir agreed to execute the bandits, although it was not long before capital punishment was replaced by fines.

In spite of his newfound humility, Vladimir saw himself as in no way subservient to Byzantium. Although the Russian Church was organized under a metropolitan appointed by the patriarch of Constantinople, it was the grand prince who set the pace of its development and determined the extent of its authority. Without his patronage and support, the Church would have been incapable of carrying out its mission—a fact that was certainly not lost on the Greeks.

Even with Vladimir's support, the preaching of the infant Church more often led to cracked skulls than saved souls. Loyalty to the old gods died hard, and resistance to conversion, particularly among the rural population, was widespread. The Church hardly added to its appeal by trying to ban such supposed manifestations of paganism as singing, dancing, and even laughing. Nor was its popularity enhanced by its repeated attacks on sexual promiscuity, a phenomenon which seems to have been rarely absent from a Russian feast or festival. These denunciations seem to have had at best a limited effect, for two and a half centuries later the Kievan metropolitan Cyril was still addressing the problem in passionate terms: "On Saturday evening men and women come together, play and dance shamelessly, and indulge in obscenities on the night of the Holy Resurrection, just as ungodly pagans celebrating the feast of Dionysus; men and women together, like horses, frolic and neigh and make obscenities. . . . And now let them cease."

Spearheading the opposition to the Church were the *volkhvi,* heathen magicians who helped to keep alive the old faith and stirred up opposition to the clergy. In its entry for the year 1071, the *Primary Chronicle* mentions a violent uprising in the lower Volga region in which "the common people all followed the volkhvi." The most enthusiastic of the Church's supporters were the princes and their retinues, who welcomed its pronouncements on the social order as a divine justification of their own powers and privileges. Their views were well expressed in the words of the *Hundred Chapters,* an apocryphal text popular in Russia at the time: "Bow your head to everybody senior to you. . . . Fear the prince with all your power. . . . From him you will learn how to fear God. . . . Who does not fear the earthly lord, how will he fear Him who he does not see?" However, political self-interest was not the only consideration, and many of the Kievan elite were as eager as Vladimir himself to receive the cultural benefits of Byzantium.

A key factor in the Church's success was the decision to address the people of the Kievan state in their own Slav tongue. In this the Church was following in the footsteps of the two original apostles to the Slavs, Saints Cyril and Methodius, Greek missionary brothers responsible for the conversion of the Moravians in the ninth century. Wishing to make the gospel more accessible to their flock, the brothers

Bench

Lobby

Stove

Established in the tenth century on the Volkhov River, the city of Novgorod was the most important trading center in northern Russia. Although the city owed nominal allegiance to the grand prince of Kiev, control effectively lay in the hands of the townsfolk, represented by an influential town council that ran municipal affairs. A powerful and independently minded merchant class, living in its own quarter, enriched the city with the fruits of trade with Germany and Scandinavia. The town was so highly regarded by its own citizens that they styled it "Lord Novgorod the Great."

Living in a thickly forested region, the Novgorodians naturally chose wood as their main building material. A typical house *(inset)* took the form of a square or rectangle, partitioned across one end to form a lobby. The living space was furnished with wide benches that served both as shelves and as bunk beds. Heat was supplied by a large clay stove, the smoke from which escaped through a hatch in the roof. Windows consisted of simple shuttered slots set between the pine logs that composed the walls.

Outside, staves of pine were used to form fences and entrance porches. Even the streets were surfaced with pine logs, halved lengthwise and laid flat-side down.

Fire was a constant menace in this wooden world, but when it struck, rebuilding was rapid: A gutted house could be replaced in a single day. Such resilience ensured that Novgorod survived most assaults, to become in later centuries the capital of the richest state in Russia.

adopted an existing Slavic alphabet—since known as the Cyrillic script—and produced the first Slavic translations of the scriptures and liturgies. Though based on the dialect of southern Bulgaria, the language of these translations, known appropriately as Church Slavonic, was quite comprehensible to the Kievans, and it was to remain the literary language of Russia until the eighteenth century.

Nevertheless, Russia's inheritance from the cultural treasure house of Byzantium was only a fraction of the available riches: For the establishment of Church Slavonic as the country's liturgical language meant that Russian scholars had no necessity to learn Greek or Latin, an omission that cut them off from the cultural heritage of classical learning passed on to the rest of Europe. Still, Byzantium had much to offer, and it was in the visual arts—church architecture, icon painting, the designing of religious frescoes and mosaics—that Byzantine influence was most evident. The main beneficiary was Kiev, which by the time of Vladimir's death, in 1015, had been transformed from a crude frontier town into a cultivated metropolis. One contemporary observer wrote that the city had eight great marketplaces and forty churches.

Vladimir had fought for the throne against his own brothers, and following his death, his sons engaged in a similar struggle. Early success went to Prince Sviatopolk, who seized Kiev and had three of his rivals murdered. Two of them, Boris and Gleb, refusing to resist evil with evil, submitted to their assassins and became the first Russians to be canonized. Another of the brothers, Yaroslav of Novgorod, proved less willing to turn the other cheek, and after twenty-one years of intermittent strife, it was he who emerged as the undisputed ruler of the Kievan state. By now, ten of his eleven brothers were dead. Sudislav, the surviving brother, was imprisoned by Yaroslav in 1035, and in prison Sudislav was to remain for the next quarter of a century.

It was under Yaroslav, known as the Wise, that Kievan Russia reached the summit of its achievement. He began his reign with a resounding victory over the Pechenegs, sweeping them off the southern steppe and restoring the security of Kiev's vital trade route to the Black Sea. (The Pechenegs were to be replaced by an even more fearsome group of nomads, but not until after Yaroslav's death.) With the threat from the south removed, Yaroslav was content to live largely at peace with neighboring states,

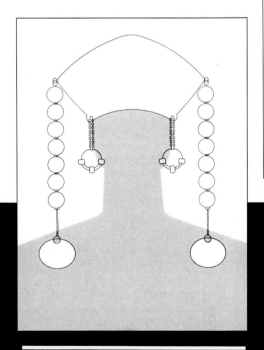

Crescent-shaped *kolty,* or temple rings, were worn as adornments by both sexes of the Russian aristocracy, probably for weddings and other festive occasions. Made from gold or silver and sometimes encircled with pearls, the rings were hung from headbands or else suspended on chains from ceremonial headdresses *(above).* Originally connected with a pagan moon cult, they continued in use into Christian times, when the enameled decorations they bore often reflected images drawn from both religions.

A Christian saint is represented fullface and haloed, in the Byzantine manner.

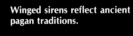

Winged sirens reflect ancient pagan traditions.

relying on a series of dynastic marriages to bolster his power and prestige.

His own wedding to Ingigerda, daughter of King Olaf, linked him to the Swedish royal house, and through the nuptials that he arranged for his sisters and his children, he also forged close ties with the ruling families of Poland, Norway, Hungary, France, and Byzantium. In the eyes of foreign rulers, Kievan Russia was now a great power—a fact proclaimed as much by its style as by its strength. For example, at the wedding, in 1051, of Yaroslav's daughter Anna to Henry I of France, the young Kievan princess was able to sign her name, whereas her illiterate groom could only make an *X*.

Determined to turn Kiev into a second Constantinople, Yaroslav embarked on a lavish building program, endowing his capital with an imposing new fortress and still more churches. So impressed with the city was the German chronicler Adam of Bremen that he described it as "the fairest jewel" in all the Greek Orthodox world. Its focal point was the sumptuous Cathedral of Saint Sophia, the marble for which Yaroslav had imported from Byzantium. There the grand prince, a confirmed bibliophile, assembled scribes and translators to create the first Russian library.

Yaroslav also issued the first Russian legal code, Russkaya Pravda (The Russian Law), which was based in large part on Slavic traditional law. Unlike the harsh legal code of Byzantium, with its emphasis on corporal and capital punishment, the Pravda contained no provisions for the death penalty (although it permitted the killing of robbers caught in the act) and prescribed beating for only one offense—the striking of a freeman by a slave. All other crimes and misdemeanors were to be dealt with through the payment of fines and compensation, though in the case of murder, the Pravda reaffirmed the ancient right of blood vengeance, prescribing a fine, or bloodwite, only where there was no kinsman to avenge the victim.

Under Yaroslav's code, all freemen were equal before the law, and every murder incurred the same bloodwite—forty *grivna* (thought to be equivalent to about ninety-five ounces of silver). However, equality was soon replaced by class distinction, and under the Pravda of Yaroslav's sons, issued around 1072, the bloodwite varied according to the social status of the victim. Thus, it was increased to eighty grivna for the murder of a princely official but was only five grivna for the murder of a peasant.

At the top of the social pyramid stood the grand prince of Kiev and his relatives, the princes of the cities and territories beyond Kiev; then came the boyars, powerful landowners who had received their estates as a reward for past services to various princes of the ruling dynasty and who made up the governing elite of Kievan Russia. However, unlike the feudal lords of western Europe, who were in theory at least bound by bonds of vassalage to a particular ruler, the boyars were free to give their allegiance to whichever prince seemed to offer the best prospects. Moreover, a boyar retained the land granted to him by one prince even if he chose to enter the realm and service of another.

The same right of free movement applied at the lower end of the social order, to the free peasantry—smallholders with their own land, farming implements, and animals. Instead of being tied to the estate of a hereditary lord, they were able to come and go as they pleased and could pass their holdings on to their heirs. However, whereas a boyar without male heirs could bequeath his property to a daughter, a peasant in the same situation would have his property taken over by the local ruler.

A more immediate problem for the peasant was likely to be shortage of money. Even at the best of times he was hard pressed to make a living, but when times were bad—after a crop failure, for example, or following the imposition of a particularly

Two birds flank a stylized image of the Tree of Life.

heavy tax by the prince—he could be forced to sacrifice his independence and join the ranks of the despised *zakupi*. These were debtors who had contracted to pay off their loans through service rather than money. Though still technically freemen, the zakupi had to do whatever work was required of them, and if they tried to escape, they became the permanent slaves of their creditors.

Yaroslav died in 1054, and with his death began the inexorable decline of Kievan Russia. According to the custom, Yaroslav had arranged for the realm to be divided between his heirs in order of seniority. Thus, his eldest son received Novgorod and Kiev; his second son, Chernigov; and so on down to his fifth son, who was given the outlying region of Volhynia, on the border with Poland. The arrangement was intended to avoid dynastic conflict. However, it had failed to work following the deaths of Yaroslav's father and grandfather, and it failed to work following Yaroslav's own death. Instead, the country was plunged into a state of almost continuous civil war as successive generations of princes maneuvered and battled for power. In their struggles, they often turned for help to the latest wave of barbarian invaders from the east—known to the Russians as Polovtsi, but to themselves as Kipchaks—who, besides involving themselves in the nation's internal power struggles, also raided across the southern frontiers almost at will, looting and burning villages and killing or enslaving the local population.

Occasionally, the princes managed to suspend their own quarreling long enough to fight the common enemy, and there was even a period, from 1113 to 1125, when the country was reunited under the charismatic leadership of the grand prince Vladimir Monomakh, a grandson of Yaroslav. However, after Vladimir's death, the feuding flared up with renewed venom. In 1196, Kiev itself, "the mother of Russian cities," was captured and pillaged—not by a foreign invader, but by a faction of Russian princes under Andrei Bogolyubsky of Suzdal. Although Andrei eagerly assumed the title of grand prince, he gave the city to a young brother, preferring to keep his own capital at Vladimir, in the northeast.

The fact was that the focus of Russian life was shifting northward, to Vladimir, to Suzdal, to Novgorod, and in the course of time, to Moscow. Kiev had owed its preeminence to its strategic position on the great trade route from the Baltic to the Black Sea. But that conduit was losing its reason for existence. For centuries, it had remained vital to Byzantium because of the stranglehold exerted by the Muslims on the more direct path to western Europe, via the Mediterranean. However, in the course of the twelfth century, the Muslims were forced to loosen their grip, with the result that more and more goods were sent by way of the Mediterranean, and fewer and fewer by way of "the road from the Varangians to the Greeks." The final blow to Kiev's commerce came in 1204, when the warriors of the Fourth Crusade, instead of liberating the Holy Land, conquered and sacked Constantinople.

New enemies made their presence felt to the west, but it was from the east that the fatal challenge was to come—from the Mongols. In 1237 and again in 1240, these most terrible of all invaders would smash their way across the Volga River in two devastating campaigns that were to bring about the final collapse of Kievan Russia. Two more centuries were to pass before the emergence of its successor, and when the principality of Muscovy finally appeared in the fifteenth century as a nucleus from which a Russian state could again grow, it was to be a very different nation that developed, more isolated and more autocratic than the prosperous and surprisingly free land that Yaroslav the Wise had ruled from his splendid capital of Kiev.

CITADELS OF THE SPIRIT

In an age of deep religious commitment, the followers of many faiths sought to express their devotion by building monumental places of worship. Working in radically different cultural traditions, architects all over the world, from Mayan America to Islamic Egypt, Christian Europe to Hindu India, planned and laid out their holy sites according to their own particular beliefs and their unique vision of a divinely ordered universe.

Some of the structures served to house the divinity. To the Hindu priests of the Kandarya Mahadeva temple in northern India, the building was both a dwelling place for the god Shiva and a symbolic microcosm of the created world. Similarly, the pagoda of Ying Xian in northern China represented in its layout a diagram of the universe in miniature and invoked the omnipresence of the Buddha.

In other religions, the principal purpose of holy places was to focus attention on the eternal through prayer. The al-Hakim Mosque in Cairo was a communal meeting place for its Muslim worshipers, who held the belief that God could be approached without resort to any special artifice, because he was present everywhere and in all things. The Christian monks of Jumièges in Normandy hoped to lead their congregation to salvation through the public celebration of Mass as well as by individual acts of devotion.

For the Mayan civilization of Mexico's Yucatán peninsula, religion was insepara-

1 AL-HAKIM MOSQUE

2 EL CASTILLO STEP PYRAMID

3 KANDARYA MAHADEVA TEMPLE

4 JUMIÈGES ABBEY CHURCH

5 YING XIAN PAGODA

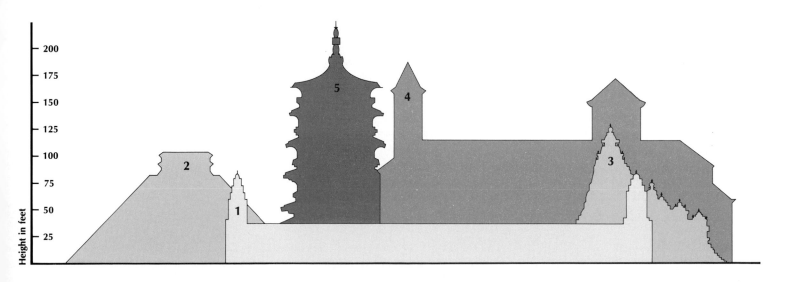

ble from politics, saturating the whole fabric of life and defining each individual's status. The highly stratified nature of Mayan society was expressed in concrete terms by the temple of El Castillo at Chichén Itzá, a square pyramid mounting in steps from a huge base to a small temple. Here, on the temple platform, a public theater of blood was frequently enacted, with the priesthood offering animal and human sacrifices in return for divine favors, and the awed populace gathered below to act out the role of spectators.

To a greater or lesser extent, all these structures served a political function as well as a religious purpose. While they honored the supernatural, they also celebrated the power and munificence of the earthly rulers who had ordered, and sometimes paid for, their construction.

Yet above all, these buildings bore witness to a belief in powers greater and more permanent than the human authority of king or emperor. They were testaments to an age of faith.

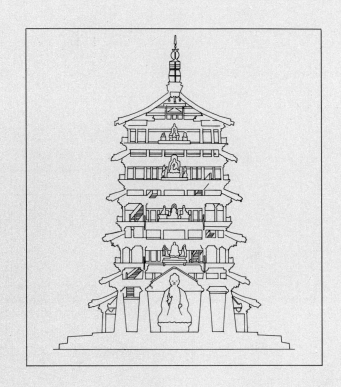

A CELESTIAL TOWER

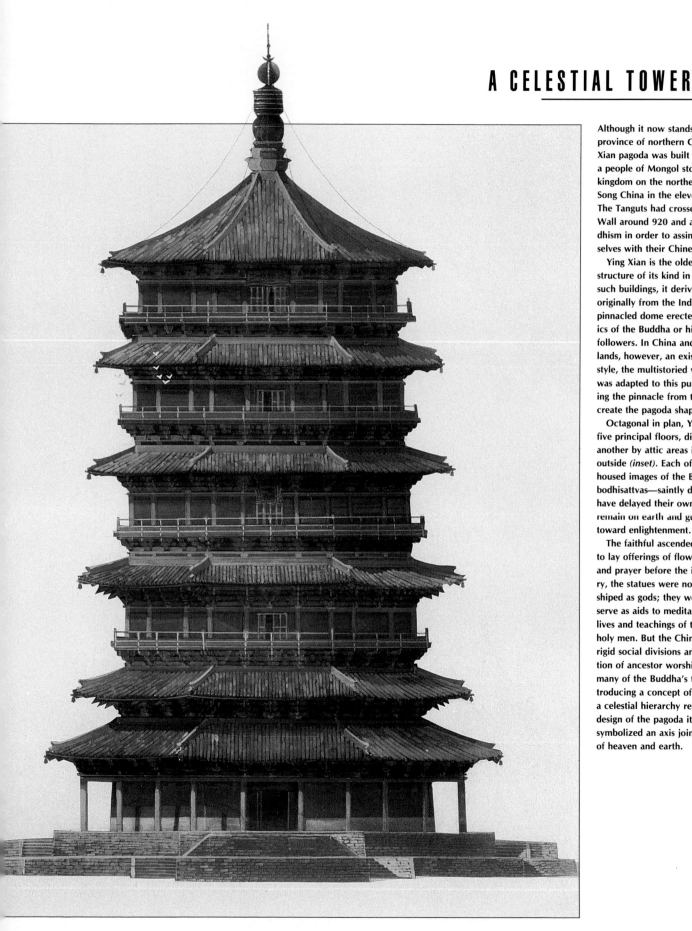

Although it now stands in the Shansi province of northern China, the Ying Xian pagoda was built by the Tanguts, a people of Mongol stock who ruled a kingdom on the northern borders of Song China in the eleventh century. The Tanguts had crossed the Great Wall around 920 and adopted Buddhism in order to assimilate themselves with their Chinese subjects.

Ying Xian is the oldest wooden structure of its kind in China. Like all such buildings, it derives its function originally from the Indian stupa—a pinnacled dome erected to house relics of the Buddha or his most devout followers. In China and neighboring lands, however, an existing building style, the multistoried watchtower, was adapted to this purpose, preserving the pinnacle from the stupa to create the pagoda shape.

Octagonal in plan, Ying Xian had five principal floors, divided one from another by attic areas invisible from outside *(inset)*. Each of the main levels housed images of the Buddha and his bodhisattvas—saintly disciples who have delayed their own salvation to remain on earth and guide humankind toward enlightenment.

The faithful ascended these stories to lay offerings of flowers, incense, and prayer before the images. In theory, the statues were not to be worshiped as gods; they were meant to serve as aids to meditation upon the lives and teachings of the Buddhist holy men. But the Chinese, with their rigid social divisions and their tradition of ancestor worship, modified many of the Buddha's teachings, introducing a concept of an earthly and a celestial hierarchy reflected in the design of the pagoda itself, which symbolized an axis joining the centers of heaven and earth.

A THEATER OF BLOOD

In Mexico's Yucatán peninsula, the El Castillo step pyramid was the centerpiece of Chichén Itzá, a holy city of the Mayan civilization controlled by priests and maintained by the forced labor of the local peasantry. The principal gods in the traditional Mayan pantheon were associated with the forces of nature and creation, and since Yucatán was an arid, sunbaked land, the greatest boons to be requested of these deities were rain, fertility, and a plentiful harvest of corn.

At rainmaking ceremonies, priests burned a kind of resin that gave off thick black smoke in simulation of rain clouds. To calculate the appropriate times for planting and ritual, the Maya relied on the outstanding knowledge of their astronomers, who had developed a remarkably sophisticated system of timekeeping. El Castillo itself was designed partly as an architectural diagram of the calendar; its four flights of steps each comprised 91 steps, 364 in all, to which was added one more, up to the temple's sanctum, for a total number equal to that of the solar year.

Around the year 1000, Yucatán was invaded by the Itzá tribe, who brought with them the cult of a feathered serpent god and the practice of human sacrifice, learned from the Toltecs of northern Mexico. At rainmaking ceremonies and other major sacrificial rites, worshipers assembled at the base of the temple, while nobles drew barbed thongs through their own tongues and ears, spilling their blood onto pieces of bark for presentation to the gods. Above them in the sanctum, children tied to the altar raised their voices in imitation of frogs, whose croaking heralded the coming of rain. Gorgeously attired priests divided into different orders officiated at the ceremonies. One order held the arms and legs of the victims—often prisoners of war—while another split open their chests with flints to pluck out their hearts. The lifeless bodies were then hurled down the pyramid steps and submerged, together with offerings of gold, jade, and copper, in a nearby well.

A PLACE FOR COMMUNAL PRAYER

Cairo's al-Hakim Mosque took its name from the sixth Fatimid caliph of Egypt, who presided over its completion in 1013. An eccentric noted for his persecution of Christians and Jews, he subsequently became convinced of his own divinity. He disappeared under mysterious circumstances in 1021 and has been held ever since by the Druse communities of the Middle East to have been an incarnation of God.

At the time that the mosque was built, however, he was a fierce proponent of the Shiite branch of Islam. The prophet Muhammad, founder of the Islamic faith, had decreed an austere monotheism and forbidden his followers to construct, or to worship, religious images. The only decorations allowed in the mosque, therefore, were geometrical designs and phrases, in beautifully executed calligraphy, from Islam's holy book, the Koran.

In its layout, the al-Hakim Mosque —like all others—was modeled on Muhammad's own house in the Arabian town of Mecca. The open courtyard *(inset)*, containing nothing more than a fountain for the ritual ablutions that preceded prayer, was large enough to accommodate half the male population of Cairo; women were excluded from public worship. Around the courtyard were arcaded aisles that served as meeting places for the study and exposition of the Koran.

As in all mosques, an arched niche called the mihrab was constructed in the wall facing Mecca to orient worship toward Muhammad's birthplace. The faithful visited the mosque daily; the largest turnout was on Fridays, when attendance was compulsory and a sermon was preached. An imam, or prayer leader, guided their devotions, after an official known as the muezzin had summoned the congregation from the top of a minaret with the cry, "There is no God but Allah, and Muhammad is his prophet." The al-Hakim Mosque, unusually, boasted two such minarets, both relatively massive in form as the original columns were found to need buttressing soon after their completion.

MIHRAB

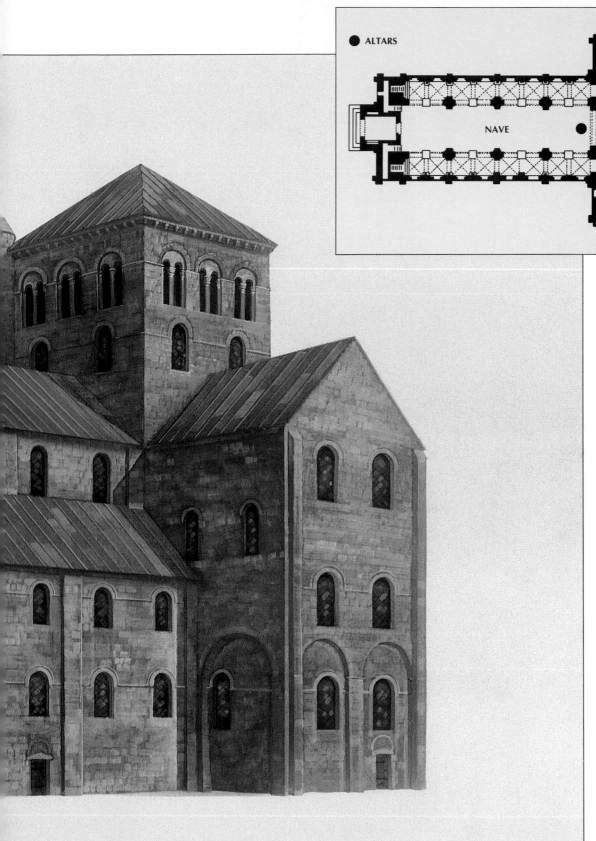

ALTARS

NAVE · CHOIR ● SANCTUARY

After thirty years of construction, the abbey church of Jumièges was dedicated in 1067 in the presence of Duke William of Normandy, recently returned to his homeland from the conquest of England.

In plan, Jumièges followed the traditional cross shape *(inset),* symbolic of Christ's crucifixion. To the west stretched the nave, terminating in two great towers marking the main entrance. This was the public part of the church, where the Benedictine monks who served the building held processions and the laity attended Mass, standing or kneeling in prayer.

A screen separated the laity from the eastern end of the building, consisting of the sanctuary and the choir, where the monks conducted the offices. Only important dignitaries, such as the duke and his male relatives, were allowed inside the sanctuary.

The windows that pierced the walls of Jumièges were relatively small. But though the interior received little daylight, the gloom was relieved by the flames of candles, the glint of gold and silver metalwork, and a variety of textiles and paintings depicting the life of Christ and the saints.

'WOMB HOUSE'

Dedicated to the Hindu god Shiva, the eleventh-century Kandarya Mahadeva temple was built as part of the Khajraho complex in north-central India. In accordance with Hindu custom, the temple site was chosen and prepared with care. Brahmans, priests of the highest social caste, would have banished the native spirits of the locality before planting the 'seed' of the building—a casket from which the temple was believed to germinate in the same way as a living organism.

Deliberately constructed to imitate the peaks and valleys of a sacred mountain, Kandarya Mahadeva owed the richness of its exterior texture to more than 900 carvings of gods, animals, dancing girls, and demons. Pilgrims entered its darkened interior to make offerings of flowers and oil at shrines dedicated to the consort of the patron deity. Repeating a soundless prayer that they be led from illusion to reality, death-in-life to immortality, the faithful pursued a ritual clockwise movement toward a central pillared hall *(inset)*. From here it was possible to make out, but not approach, the holy of holies, the 'womb house,' which at Kandarya Mahadeva housed a marble lingam, symbol of Shiva, potency, and the life force. Even in the near darkness the walls were decorated with intricate carvings, often of an erotic nature since Hindus held the sexual act to symbolize the unity of the cosmos.

On the outside, above the shrine, towered the sikhara, the highest peak of the stone mountain. When a newly built temple was to be consecrated, a priest would climb to the top of this spire and pierce it to create an aperture, representing the eye of the temple opening to the celestial sphere.

INDIA'S ELEPHANT KINGS

South India had known nothing like it: block upon granite block, carried by barge and oxcart to the new imperial capital, then hewn and carved and painfully erected into a gigantic temple that was as massive in its bulk as it was intricate in its detail. This impressive structure was dedicated to Shiva, Hinduism's god of both destruction and renewal; but the inscriptions that adorned the temple's enormous plinth declared to the world in the complex whirls and curlicues of the southern Indian Tamil script the power as well as the piety of Shiva's mightiest worshiper. Rajaraja Chola, the Great, the King of Kings, was well served by his master masons. Let those who could read, read of his achievements; those who could not, who had merely eyes to see, let them look upon the great stone pinnacle that towered above the city of Tanjore and gasp in amazement at the Chola splendor. For South India had known nothing like the Chola empire, either.

When the temple was completed, in the year 1010 as Christians would reckon time, the golden finial that marked the apex of its tremendous stepped pyramid looked down upon a vast courtyard, fronted with smaller shrines to lesser divinities, and pillared halls where devotees and pilgrims could shelter from the summer sun or the lashing rain of the monsoons. Beyond the granite enclosure stretched a large and thriving city, a cosmopolitan capital to which traders made their way from all over Asia. Tanjore's artisans, working in copper, brass, and above all, bronze, had won an international reputation—the interior of the great temple was a showcase of their finest work—and its jewelers were almost as renowned. Merchants, organized in guilds and corporations, traded with their fellows throughout the Chola domains and beyond, for Arabs, Malays, and the occasional Chinese were among those who came to barter or pay gold and silver for the region's ebony and ivory, its spices and finely worked cotton.

And the wealth circulated. Rajaraja had endowed his great temple munificently—with more than 550 pounds of gold and more of silver, some records claimed, not to mention innumerable jewels and the title to impressive estates. Wealthy guilds and families sought to emulate their royal master by establishing temples of their own. The temples in turn became customers and markets for the city's luxury products and large-scale employers of tradespeople, from goldsmiths to musicians. The great temple alone absorbed the services of hundreds of priests and other attendants, including 400 sacred prostitutes, who devoted their bodies to the service of the gods and who had two streets to house them, as well as the thousands of agricultural laborers who tended the temple's fields.

Tanjore was a city of learning too. Students at its schools and colleges studied the classics of the Hindu religion in their original language, Sanskrit, as well as the great literature of the south in the native Tamil tongue. On a lower level, clerks diligently

Cast in bronze, a Hindu deity and his attendant survey the world from an elephant's back. The statuette dates from the Chola period of Indian history, when the Tamil-speaking people of that name built a great empire under the rule of two renowned warrior-kings, Rajaraja and Rajendra.

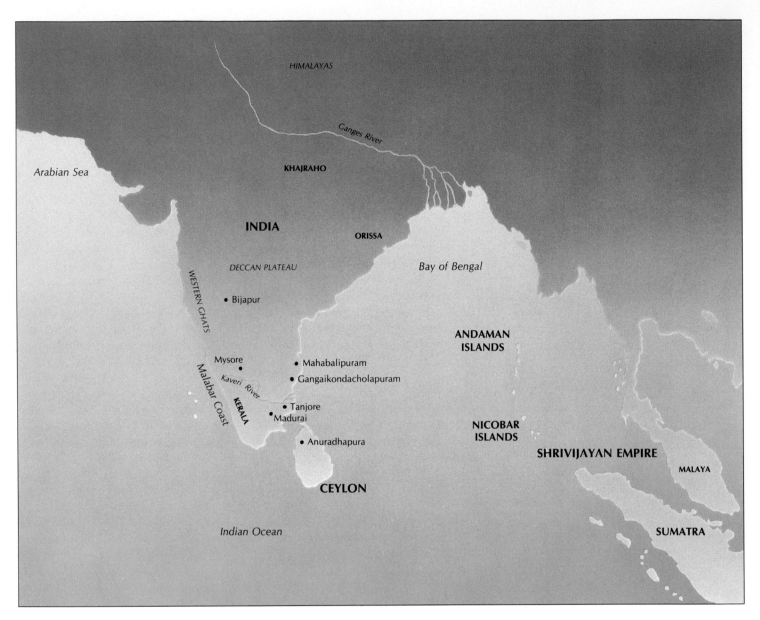

and carefully inscribed all legal transactions, land grants, and edicts on sheaves of copperplates, thereby providing an underpinning for the complex Chola legal system and leaving for posterity a collection of records almost as durable as Rajaraja's magnificent temple itself.

If it had been possible to climb to the top of the temple tower (in fact its capstone was a solid granite dome weighing eighty-five tons or more, and not a viewing gallery) visitors could have seen for themselves the source of Chola wealth and power. It was not to be found in the city, although Tanjore was the glittering expression of both riches and empire; nor even in the lucrative trade that flowed along the roads leading from the capital—east to the ports on the Bay of Bengal less than sixty-five miles away, west toward the distant mountain range of the Western Ghats, south to the old city of Madurai and beyond, and north, where Chola dominion was edging its way upward through the Deccan Plateau.

The land itself, the vast shallow valley terrain of South India, was the Cholas' great resource. Around Tanjore, the many branches of the Kaveri River trickled sluggishly toward the sea through a countryside of palms and bananas, stained here and there with the deep, intransigent green of a stand of uncleared forest. The dominant feature, though, was the endless checkerboard of low embankments outlining the paddy fields where twice or even three times annually the waters of the Kaveri, brought under control and diverted in an age beyond the reach of memory, drew from the rich, red earth the young rice seedlings, green as emeralds, that nourished the land's people and sustained its power.

As far as history records—and chronicles are often vague and ambiguous, when they exist at all—the agrarian civilization of southern India has always been based on the river valleys. In June and October, twice-yearly monsoons bring generous rainfall, not only swelling the rivers, but enriching them with upstream forest nutrients. They could also bring devastating floods; but from very early times, cultivators learned, by draining and channeling, to control at least in part the rising waters. In the course of the centuries, they even managed to extend the boundaries of cultivation, building new irrigation works in the drier plains and uplands that were found between the branches of the river.

As these farmers expanded their settlements, they came into contact with a different breed of men, fierce hunter-warriors who were strangers to regulated agricultural existence. The cultivators feared these nomads, turning for protection from them to warrior-chieftains who could offer military security. So kings made their appearance: leaders who first would tame the hill peoples in combat, then in the course of time recruit some of them to serve as soldiers. A few of the nomads even settled to agriculture, expanding further the frontiers of rice; others kept to their old ways, hostile and unreconciled.

Sheer distance spared the people of the south from the Aryan invasions that changed the north of the subcontinent in the middle of the second millennium BC. In their far-off valley kingdoms they were able to maintain their own distinct culture against foreign inroads, and they also preserved their language, Tamil and its relatives, from the Indo-European Sanskrit that the Aryans made the dominant tongue elsewhere. But they were not immune to the powerful religious and cultural influence spreading from the north, and by the time their written history begins, more than a thousand years after the Aryan conquests, southerners worshiped many of the same gods as the northern invaders.

In their southern fastnesses, the early kingdoms had, at best, loose and shifting boundaries. Rulers jostled among themselves for temporary dominance, alternately achieving and submitting to some form of overlordship. Communication between valleys was poor, and it was hard for even the mightiest local ruler to project his authority any great distance or for any great length of time. It was into this fluid and uncertain world, in which ruling houses continually rose, wavered, and fell, sometimes absorbing one another through intermarriage, sometimes fighting one another to destruction, that the Chola kingdom was born.

The exact origins of the dynasty and the people who shared its name are lost in the mists of prehistory. What is known is that kings calling themselves Cholas were a part

The Chola kingdom was based in the valley of the Kaveri River in southeastern India. From their capital of Tanjore, the Chola monarchs carried their dominion westward as far as the Malabar Coast and northward to the Deccan. In the 1020s, Rajendra annexed the island of Ceylon and sent an expeditionary force to blaze a trail of conquest as far as the Ganges River; in the following decade, he launched an assault on the Shrivijaya empire, centered on the island of Sumatra, 1,200 miles away across the Indian Ocean.

of South India from the earliest recorded times. An inscription of the great northern emperor Asoka—who controlled for a brief period more of the subcontinent than anyone before modern times—counts the Cholas among the emperor's friends, though not his subjects; the inscription dates from the third century BC and implies that the Cholas were not newcomers even then. Four hundred years later, they were important enough to be mentioned by the Greek geographer Ptolemy, who lived in the Mediterranean city of Alexandria, half a world away.

But the first truly vivid picture of the Cholas comes in the early centuries of the Christian era with the immense, creative explosion of Tamil literature known as the Shangam Age. According to Tamil tradition, there were three Shangams, great assemblies in which all the poets of the south met to pool their talents. But although the gods themselves attended the first, and the second was credited with compiling a grammar of the Tamil tongue, only the labors of the third have survived. In actual fact, the 2,000 or so extant poems—many of them of epic length—were probably composed in batches between the second and fifth centuries AD. However they were produced, the Shangam verses not only staked a claim for Tamil as one of the oldest and greatest of world literatures, they also celebrated the achievements of the Cholas and their competitors.

For there were many rivals: The Shangam epics tell of glorious, aristocratic combat between Chola kings and their neighbors, fought out by warrior bands equipped with elephants and chariots as well as lances, swords, and bows. If a king won, then after some profitable looting, he and his men retired to his palace to celebrate their triumph with a colossal banquet washed down with great quantities of palm-wine toddy served, according to one bard, by "beautiful women decked in fine jewels and sweet smiles." If he lost, but died bravely, he would be long remembered in the songs of the survivors. Poets proffered advice for those individuals seeking a military career: "When you see a fight, rush to the front, divide your enemy's forces, stand before them, and get your body scarred by the deep cuts of their swords; thus [your fame is] pleasant to the ear, not your body to the eye. As for your enemies, when they see you, they turn their backs, and with bodies whole and unscarred, they are pleasant to the eye, not so [their infamy] to the ear." One unfortunate victim, a king, was so shamed by the wound he received in his back that to redeem his honor he ultimately starved himself to death.

The world described in the poems was a sensual one. One Shangam scribe wrote lovingly of "unctuous chops of meat, cooled after boiling and soft as the carded cotton of the spinning woman"; another complained that "by eating flesh day and night, the edges of my teeth became blunt like the plowshare [after] plowing dry land." Yet even as the poets were engaged in writing, others of learning were bringing to the region newer and more ascetic ideas from the north. A trickle of Aryan Brahmans, respected for their scholarship and piety, preached more refined ideas of caste, ritual, and indeed, diet than the Shangam world had previously known. In the north, the Brahmans had developed a full caste system, assigning all human beings to hereditary caste groups or condemning them to outcaste status. These groups were maintained by an ingrained fear of pollution, which meant that they could neither eat together nor intermarry.

In practice, society was not quite so rigid as this delineation of the caste system suggests; but these notions were gladly received by southern India's ruling dynasties, for they stressed the special status attached to the higher castes. Divided from the

Chola commerce and sea power alike depended on frail-seeming ships that sometimes carried up to 200 passengers. Driven along by bamboo sails mounted on three or four masts and steered by means of quarter-side-rudders, such ships traded westward to Arabia and eastward to Indonesia and beyond. The boats were built without nails, because Indian engineers believed that a vessel studded with iron would be fatally attracted to magnetic rocks. Instead, they sewed the teak hull planks with cord wound from coconut fiber. The result was a tough, resilient oceangoing vessel that flexed in heavy weather and was easy to repair with everyday materials.

Chola worship centered on the Hindu deity Shiva, the benevolent god of destruction and renewal with whom most southern Indian temples were associated. Pictured below with his consort, Parvati, Shiva was most typically represented as Nataraja, "Lord of the Dance" *(opposite)*. Inside a circle of flame, the god whirls in a cosmic dance, his visage calm and unmoved as he spins between life and death in an eternal promise of release and rebirth. To produce such statues, artisans in the Chola capital of Tanjore used a technique almost as complex as the religious ideas they illustrated: the so-called lost-wax method, in which a wax original, enclosed in baked clay, was replaced by molten bronze. When the metal cooled, the clay was chipped away to reveal a perfect, finished sculpture.

common people by the observance of complex and often expensive rituals as well as by Hindu theory, the one-time warrior-chieftains could put their brigandish past behind them and think of themselves as an authentic aristocracy. In return, the Brahmans and their descendants received protection, high status, and a share in the wealth that the aristocrats could command.

A king's role became more complicated than that of a mere war leader, although courage in combat remained an essential virtue. Now much play was made of the mystic bond that united ruler and ruled. The state needed a king, the poets declared, in the same way that a body needed a head; each was part of one entity, and neither could survive in isolation. "Though blessed in every other way," wrote one, "it avails nothing to a land if there be no peace between the people and the king."

The epics depicted their ideal of kingship in the legendary figure of Karikala Chola. He was described as a descendant of the sun, a great warrior and master statesman, wise, just, and clever. He was the terror of his enemies and a model of Hindu piety, surrounding himself with Brahmans and performing the required sacrifices with precision. He was a mighty engineer: At his command, a great dam was built at the headwaters of the Kaveri, liberating the river's vast delta from the danger of flooding and enormously increasing its wealth and population. He conquered far and wide—as far as the Himalayas, some said—and when he died his people were heartbroken. "Poor indeed is this world which has lost him," the poets wailed.

Shangam chronology, based on long-forgotten events, is almost impenetrable, and the realities that lay behind the stories of Karikala are now difficult to unravel. His deeds were perhaps those of not one but two or three real kings, who may have ruled as early as the second century AD. Some details of the poems—the Himalayan expedition, for example—were probably sheer fantasy, literary fictions conjured up for the purpose of enriching a tale. But most of the achievements credited to the great king were real enough. By the early centuries of the Christian era, the Kaveri was fully exploited; the earth was so fertile, it was said, that the amount of space an elephant needed to lie down in was land enough to adequately feed seven people. A state of sorts was functioning, relying for its revenue on the land taxes and on the customs duties imposed upon its steadily increasing trade, as well as on the pillage traditionally wrought upon weaker neighbors.

It would have seemed that by the turning of the fifth century the groundwork had been laid for greatness; but then for two or three hundred years the promise of empire went unfulfilled. A drastic political change occurred—so drastic that no coherent records survive to explain it. Powerful northern raiders may have been responsible, or possibly an upsurge of the fierce tribespeople who inhabited the region's unsettled uplands. The Cholas and most of their rivals went into deep eclipse.

The gap in the records ends some time in the seventh century. But when rice-valley civilization reemerged, as mysteriously as it had disappeared, the Cholas were no longer the paramount kings. That primary role had passed to the Pallava dynasty, based in the port-capital of Mahabalipuram, located near present-day Madras and well to the north of the Cholas' Kaveri heartland. There, for a time, the Pallavas presided over a flourishing trade with Southeast Asia and Ceylon, and spent some of their wealth on South India's first great works in stone. The coastal region abounded in massive, granitic boulders; from the living rock Pallava artists hewed monolithic shrines and temples, works that were more sculpture than architecture. The artists used the same tough stone to build a series of temples on the shore, which for more

HARNESSING BRUTE STRENGTH

All over India, elephants meant power. Panoplied for war, they gave an army's front line a brute, inhuman force that terrified its enemies and cheered the fainthearted in its own ranks. Harnessed for peace, elephants hauled massive loads. Decked out in jewels and rich clothes for parades and festivals, they awed and delighted the people and displayed a ruler's might. They even had a more macabre role: In public executions, they trampled criminals to death. To the Shiva-worshiping Chola rulers, the animals had a special attraction: They were associated with Shiva and were considered the king of beasts.

Demand for elephants was high everywhere. But they did not breed well in captivity, and for the most part they had to be caught in the wild. The most effective method required skillful organization and teamwork; upward of a thousand people were involved. Part of the work force built a strong, ditched stockade, with a funneled entrance up to 330 feet long. A hidden gate was prepared to seal the trap, while the remainder of the crew spread out over many miles in a noisy beating operation that drove wild elephants into the funnel. Flaming torches kept the elephants from charging the gate; once the herd had calmed, the business of selecting and taming the most likely specimens could begin.

than a millennium were to defy the ocean's relentless lapping at their foundations.

Pallava power was much less durable. The dynasty's downfall came at the hands of the resurgent Cholas, who had never altogether vanished from the valleys of the Kaveri. For a time, they had had to be content with Pallava overlordship—not necessarily a great hardship, for by then the Tamil ruling class, for all its squabbling, was thoroughly interbred. But with the coming of Vijayalaya Chola, about AD 850, their fortunes changed. Acting as a Pallava vassal, Vijayalaya captured the city of Tanjore on his master's behalf from a minor warrior clan. Mahabalipuram was far away, and the Pallavas had their hands full with other troublesome underkings, so Vijayalaya kept his conquest for himself. It was the start of a time of resurgence in which Vijayalaya, his son, and his grandson Parantaka worked to consolidate the Chola position. In three generations, the Cholas expanded their small, subject principality into a fair-size empire. By the mid-tenth century, the Pallavas were Chola feudatories; and so were most of the other rulers of South India.

But Chola success—and the tempting disorder their rapid expansion had brought to the Tamil country—attracted the attention of warlike outsiders from the Deccan. Parantaka beat off one attack early in his reign, but a second attempt, in the king's old age, was more successful. In a climactic battle in about the year 950, his heir was killed. In the words of one account, "The ornament of the solar race . . . was himself pierced in his heart, while seated on the back of a large elephant, by the sharp arrows of the enemy. . . . He ascended to the heaven of heroes." His army melted away, and the newly won Chola empire threatened to follow suit.

The old king died in 955. The next thirty years were an unhappy time for the dynasty. A succession of weak and short-lived kings—at least one was assassinated—struggled to hold onto what was left. But their opponents were in no better shape. As always, success in dynastic warfare encouraged overexpansion, which gave restive vassals the chance to rebel against preoccupied overlords. The wheel of fortune began to turn in favor of the Cholas once more.

Such was the way of the South Indian world when Rajaraja, after a long apprenticeship as crown prince, inherited the Chola throne in 985. His father had already reasserted Chola authority over much of the lost northern territory. Now Rajaraja struck south and west toward Kerala on India's Malabar Coast. The war forced some old rivals into Chola allegiance; it also brought a share of revenue from the lucrative Malabar trade with the Arabs, who came in white-sailed dhows to barter horses and weapons for the legendary spices of the Malabar Coast.

Kerala's rulers had been allied with the king of Ceylon, who had troubles of his own with foreign mercenaries he had hired, who had turned against him. While the king hid from the rebels in the southern forests of his island, Rajaraja seized the opportunity to launch a daring expedition. He landed on the island around the year 1000, destroyed its ancient capital of Anuradhapura, and returned safely home with shiploads of loot. It was a bold stroke, as well as a profitable one, but the expedition was a raid, not a war of conquest.

In fact, a few years after the Ceylon adventure, Rajaraja launched another campaign in the south, and there may even have been a third: Inscriptions glorifying the king's military prowess are numerous but none too precise. As well as reasserting his power in the south, Rajaraja pushed north, beyond the old Pallava territory, and northwest into the country around Mysore. An army entrusted to his son Rajendra pressed on deep into the Deccan Plateau as far as the Bijapur region, more than 400 miles from Tanjore. An inscription dating from 1007 gives the defenders' point of view: Rajendra, with 900,000 troops, "plundered the whole country, killed women, children, and Brahmans, caught hold of girls and destroyed their caste." The numbers were no doubt grossly exaggerated; there were probably far fewer fighting men in the whole subcontinent. But the fate of those in Rajendra's path, as he cut his way through the immensity of India, is likely enough. (It is only deaths of women, children, and Brahmans that his enemies held against him—everyone else was fair game or not worth mentioning.)

Rajendra had pressed too far forward and had to retire with some losses. But loot from the wars must have helped defray the cost of his father's great temple, not to mention the other expenses involved in maintaining what was already an enormous empire. There was more growth to come. In 1012, two years after the completion of the temple, Rajendra was given a formal share in the running of the state—a Chola tradition that calmed an heir's impatience and trained him in the arts of government. When his father died in 1014, the new emperor already had experience as well as ambition, and he used both background and desire to extend Chola power to the farthest geographical limits it ever attained.

In the north, he carried his authority far into the Deccan. He fought another war in Kerala. This time, his victorious armies returned to Tanjore with the regalia of the defeated king. (His father had been content with pledges of allegiance, which had been respected only when a Chola army was nearby to enforce them.) Like his father before him, Rajendra invaded Ceylon—and his attack was no mere raid, but a serious attempt to conquer the island.

It was highly successful. Ceylon's King Mahinda lost more than his regalia: The Chola army seized all his goods and sacred relics, not to mention his queen and his daughter, and the monarch himself remained a prisoner in Tanjore for the rest of his life. Chola-style temples were built on the island, and although after Mahinda's death his son headed a long-running guerrilla campaign against the Tamil conquerors, Ceylon had become virtually a Chola province.

At its closest point, Ceylon is only thirty miles from the South Indian mainland. Nevertheless, the launching of a seaborne invasion strong enough to achieve decisive results was a great feat of organization as well as of arms. Ships were very small—two or three had to be lashed together to make a platform capable of carrying a war elephant. And a few elephants at least would have been necessary, as much for morale as for military reasons. The beasts were hard to handle, but the howdah of a caparisoned war elephant was the traditional battle post of every Hindu war leader, and his troops expected it.

There would have been cavalry, too, though not much: Medieval Indians were poor horse breeders, and most animals were purchased, at great expense, from Arab traders. Most of the army were foot soldiers, crammed into merchant vessels lent or chartered for the purpose, for there was no standing navy; indeed, many of the merchants probably came themselves, in the hope of loot. But once ashore, in a land where warfare between competing chieftains was endemic, a small army with a determined leader could achieve a great deal.

Rajendra made other seaborne forays. He captured what his chroniclers called the "many ancient islands, whose old, great guard was the ocean, which makes the conches resound"—possibly the Andamans or even the Nicobars. And around 1030, he launched an astonishing raid against the Southeast Asian empire of Shrivijaya, a realm long linked to India by bonds of commerce and culture, that was centered on the island of Sumatra, 1,200 miles away across the Indian Ocean. Apart from loot, the object seems to have been to discourage Shrivijayan interference in Chola trade with China and simply to flaunt Chola power in the manner that tradition and epic literature enjoined upon Indian rulers.

There was even a word for such an exercise: *digvijaya,* meaning a bravura display of magnificence and power. Rajendra's greatest digvijaya took place on the mainland. Using the newly taken northern provinces as a springboard, he sent an expedition on an armed progress through Orissa to the sacred river Ganges, located almost 1,000 miles from the Kaveri Valley. The army brought back with it vessels brimming with holy Ganges water—carried, according to boastful Chola inscriptions, on the heads of subject kings. The river water was destined for the temple in the new capital that Rajendra was building about forty-five miles from the city of Tanjore. Rajendra called the place Gangaikondacholapuram—meaning "the city of the Chola who conquered the Ganges."

Wisely, though, he never attempted to repeat the raid nor to exert his rule over the Ganges lands. His boundaries were wide enough; even in the high noon of Chola empire, there were recognized confines to imperial power.

There were limits other than distance, of course, and there always had been. Rajendra was the mightiest Chola who had ever lived, in theory the absolute ruler of all the known world. But he had no tightly organized bureaucracy through which he could exercise his authority. Away from the Chola heartland—the Kaveri and the irrigated valleys that adjoined it—power was in the hands of local dynasties who kept almost all their own revenues, paying for the privilege by acknowledging Chola hegemony and contributing troops to Chola campaigns. Imperial edicts might insist that these dynasties' revenues were "given" to them by the grace and generosity of the emperor; the truth was that he had no real alternative. The emperor gave, but he could not take away, not if he wanted to keep his empire intact. Subordinate kings and chieftains yielded their lands to the great Chola; the great Chola granted them back again; and inscriptions written down in high Tamil rhetoric marked the transaction for posterity. As the repeated wars with the Cholas' Kerala "vassals" clearly demonstrated, however, even that nominal amount of subservience could prove to be difficult to enforce.

In the heartland itself, power was also far from centralized. The basic administration unit was the village, and every village of any size had its own assembly—an institution that dated back at least to Shangam times. These assemblies were by no means democratic (they were usually dominated by Brahmans and wealthy landowners), but they had real power, and most local affairs were in their control.

In the towns, authority was vested in the *nagaram,* a term that described something between a municipal council and a self-regulating merchants' guild. Like the village assembly, the nagaram had powers of tax collection delegated to it, not only for the Chola exchequer, but also for local purposes, which sometimes included a police force. The nagaram also regulated trade and levied fines on producers of shoddy goods, as well as managing major landholdings, which it sometimes owned in its own right. Major cities might have more than one nagaram; Tanjore had several, each responsible for an area of commercial activity as well as a district of the city.

Sensuality in Stone

The temple sculptures of medieval Hindu India shared a robust sensuality that shocked later Muslim and European visitors alike. In the north as well as the south, the buildings were less decorated with stonework than clothed in ranks of statuary.

Such work was nowhere better executed than at Khajraho in north-central India, where in the tenth and eleventh centuries the Chandela dynasty flourished. Like their Chola counterparts in Tanjore, the Chandelas were lavish with their endowments. The result was no fewer than seven great temples in an area of a few square miles—a sandstone canvas on which artists left a vibrant picture of the times.

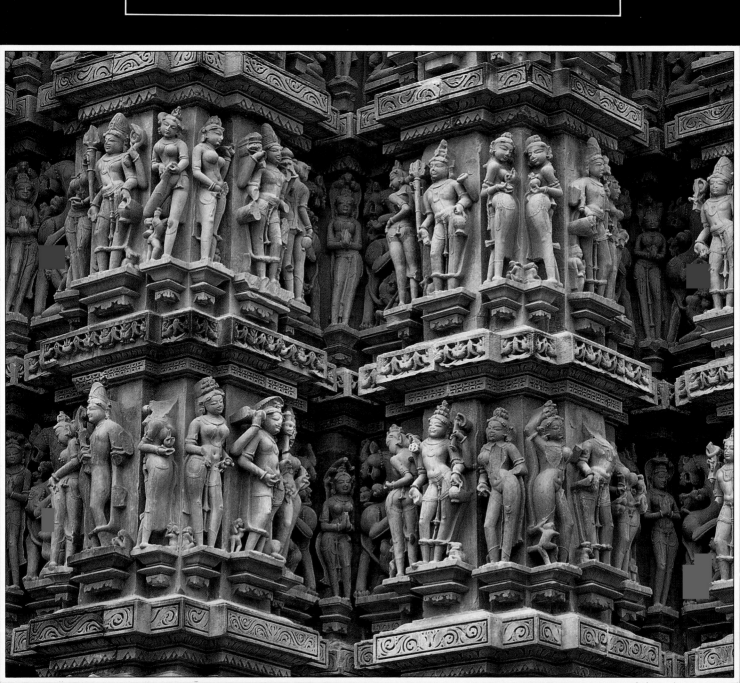

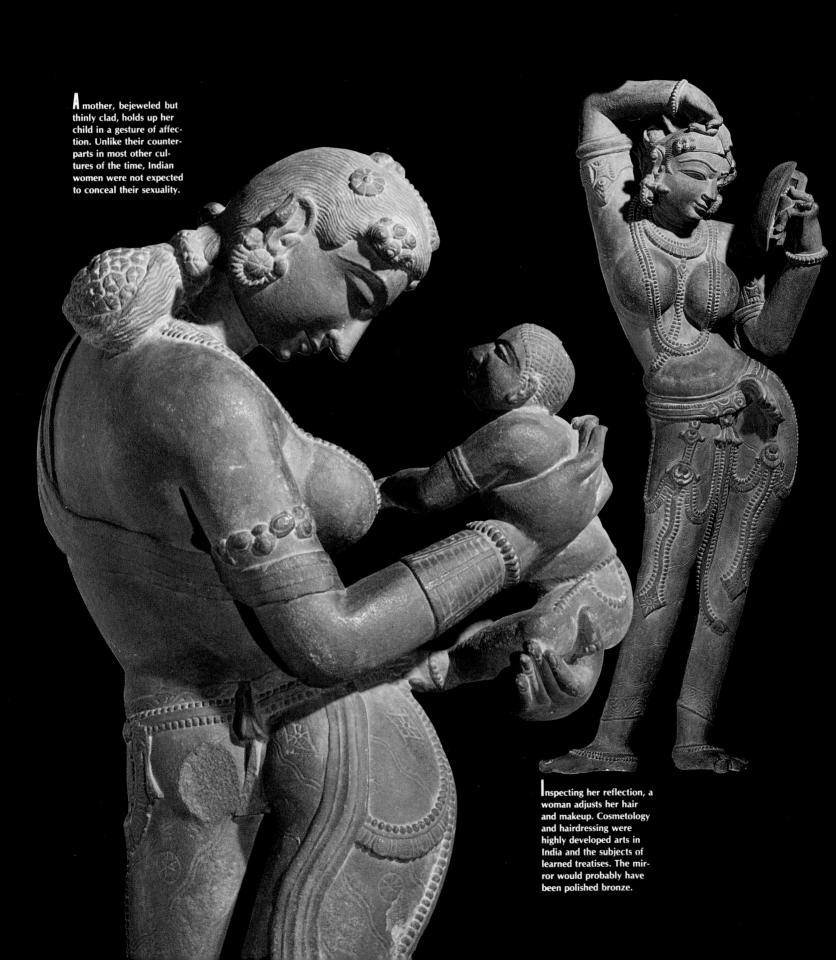

A mother, bejeweled but thinly clad, holds up her child in a gesture of affection. Unlike their counterparts in most other cultures of the time, Indian women were not expected to conceal their sexuality.

Inspecting her reflection, a woman adjusts her hair and makeup. Cosmetology and hairdressing were highly developed arts in India and the subjects of learned treatises. The mirror would probably have been polished bronze.

Poised over a representation of a wax tablet, a courtly lady uses a stylus to write a love letter. Kneeling before her, a rejected suitor gestures his despair. Well-to-do Indian women were often highly literate; usually, though, only courtesans conducted love affairs in public.

With the rise of overseas and long-distance trade throughout most of the Chola period, more straightforward merchants' guilds rose to prominence. Some had international interests: The most celebrated was "The Five Hundred of the Thousand Directions in All Countries," who sold elephants and horses as well as spices and drugs, and boasted of their travels into the "six continents," probably indicating trading forays to west and southeast Asia. Others, such as "The Just Merchants," were firmly rooted in South India. All regulated trade and clung to monopolies as best they could, paying to the Chola kings tolls and duties on their wares. In return they expected protection and received it at least up to a point. To be on the safe side, though, many merchant guilds still hired bodies of mercenary soldiers, often on a semipermanent basis, as guards and escorts.

The royal army was naturally the chief military force in the land. It was built around regiments whose officers—and probably many other ranks, too—inherited their position from their fathers. The system guaranteed stability, if not efficiency: There would be no records of attempted coups d'état. Some of the troops were equipped with elephants, although a twelfth-century Chinese traveler who claimed to have counted 60,000 of the animals was probably exaggerating at least a hundredfold. Most were infantry. Like most groups in the Chola empire, each army regiment had a distinct corporate character of its own. Regiments invested in land and endowed temples as they saw fit, according to their wealth and piety.

The army was not large. Although its troops were deployed in various towns throughout the empire, there were not enough of them to guarantee the peace—the less so since they were often fighting on a far frontier. For a major campaign, it was generally possible to recruit mercenaries to swell the ranks, and villages of any size would appear to have had a militia capable at least of limited self-defense, who might join in a battle near their homes.

The Chola administrative services were minimal, too (in a modern sense, almost nonexistent). The agents responsible for collecting such taxes as were available for the central government—and most taxes seem to have been put to local use—were usually local chieftains: members of the old warrior aristocracy long since brought into Chola allegiance, not state civil servants. Here too power was diffused.

Even the empire's most ubiquitous institutions—the Hindu temples—remained, to a large extent, independent of the court. Since their greatest benefactors were the Cholas, however, they were hardly free of royal influence, not least in the deities to whom they were dedicated. All the Chola emperors were devout followers of the god Shiva, and the temples reflected that imperial orientation. Of the trinity of great Hindu gods, Brahma is the creator, Vishnu the preserver, and Shiva the destroyer. But destruction is only one of Shiva's aspects, a role he will fulfill when the universe becomes too overwhelmed with evil to continue. Meanwhile, Shiva is also the Benevolent (the literal meaning of his name) and by another paradox a god of the ascetic life as well as of music and dancing. He was a useful god for a warrior dynasty to embrace (although the great stone temples that the Cholas would leave behind them did more to celebrate his creative aspects than his destructive ones), and he remained South India's most popular deity.

Religious feeling was an important part of the cement that held Chola civilization together, but the temples had an economic and social role that was just as binding. They were immensely rich: The great temples of Tanjore and Gangaikondacholapuram led the way in the lavishness of their endowments, but every town and most villages had temples that, relatively speaking, were almost as wealthy. For reasons of policy as well as piety, Chola rulers often assigned their share of local tax revenue to these local temples, usually in perpetuity; the result was to keep the wealth (most such taxes were levied in rice or other produce, not cash) in the area that had earned it. The temple frequently acted as a bank, making finances available for development projects, such as irrigation works, and receiving investments, on which it paid interest. It also offered rudimentary types of medical services and, in the shelter it gave to beggars and the destitute, a primitive kind of social security. In times of hardship, the temple could usually provide a reserve of food and money for the community to fall back upon.

The temples were not always so disinterestedly charitable. Some were large landowners, employing in conditions close to slavery hordes of miserable laborers who were too low caste to be permitted to worship in the buildings that they served. And Hindu humanitarianism was somewhat barbed: The temples were ready and willing purchasers of those unfortunate individuals who had been forced by debt or hopeless poverty to sell themselves into slavery. Despite their occasional and evident failings, however, the religious establishments were deeply respected by rich and poor, king, lord, and slave alike.

The temples also benefited from the Chola system of justice. Under that system, a few crimes were severely punished—a thirteenth-century Chinese visitor mentioned

Compact and almost imperishable, a sheaf of engraved copper plates attached to a fist-size ring holds Chola records from the days of Rajendra in the early eleventh century. Most such inscriptions confirmed property transfers or commercial agreements; this one acknowledged a land grant to a monastery. But the details of even the most mundane transactions were usually prefaced with a sonorous description of the reigning Chola and his family. Here, the document begins, "In the lineage of the sun was born Chola," and goes on to spell out a long list of victories and conquests. But the humble received a mention, too: The plates conclude with the names of the temple engravers who prepared them.

161

flogging, beheading, and even trampling by elephant as the fate of certain unspecified criminals. But for most offenses, including even murder, the penalty was a fine, normally paid not to the royal court, but in the form of an endowment to a temple. A murderer might have to maintain the burning of a perpetual lamp in his local place of worship, for instance, a substantial fine, in fact, since the going rate for such an endowment was no less than ninety-six sheep.

Temples spent a large proportion of their income on works of art. Virtually all of them—stone sculpture, bronzework, and painting—had a religious purpose. Most of the paintings would vanish over time (though among those that survived would be a portrait of Rajaraja himself with his guru, the teacher who initiated him into the worship of Shiva), but the considerable number of statues in stone and bronze that would remain from the tenth to the thirteenth centuries would mark that period in South India as one of the great ages in world art.

The supreme achievement, however, was in architecture: Not only in Tanjore and Gangaikondacholapuram but in a dozen other southern cities, massive, profusely sculpted temples, all distinguished by the Chola masters' rare combination of simplicity and grandeur, bore witness to the considerable skill, confidence, and religious faith of their builders.

Not everyone in the Chola empire was a devotee of Shiva, however, or even a Hindu. The preserving god Vishnu had his worshipers, and there were also a few Buddhists, followers of the way of self-perfection revealed in northern India in the sixth century BC by the Buddha himself, the "Enlightened One." Buddhist beliefs had once flourished in the south; by Chola times, though, all but a handful of the doctrine's adherents had been absorbed into the Hindu cult of Vishnu. But some Buddhist temples remained, especially at the seaports, where they attracted pilgrims from Southeast Asia.

The other important religious minority bore much in common with the Buddhists: The Jains also reverence all forms of existence and believe in nonviolence, and their faith originated at about the same time. In the Pallava era, the Jains—often wealthy merchants or farmers—came close to dominating South India's religious life, at least for a brief period; but the Pallava kings, at first sympathetic to the Jains' beliefs, returned to the Hindu fold, and Jainism retreated to a subordinate position.

Both Buddhists and Jains were treated with respect by the Chola emperors, and their respective temples received the same protection and privileges as did those of the Hindus, at least on the mainland—neither Rajaraja nor Rajendra would seem to have had any hesitation in looting the wealthy Buddhist temples and monasteries that they found in Ceylon, where Buddhism was the predominant belief. But their attacks were carried out in a spirit of greed, as pillage, not of persecution. Religious tolerance was so much a pillar of Chola statecraft that ugly clashes between Shiva worshipers and Vishnu worshipers later in the empire's history were a clear symptom of the coming of the empire's end.

Tolerance, if not respect, was also extended to the animistic beliefs of the tribal peoples who survived on the empire's fringes, leading lives not much different from their ancestors in the earliest times. Orthodox Hindus muttered about foul, pagan rites and human sacrifice, but some tribal gods seem eventually to have been transformed into minor Hindu deities: Skanda, for instance, the stunted figure who features with Shiva and his consort Parvati in some of Tanjore's finest bronzework, may originally have been an outsider, a god of the warrior tribes.

The Game of Kings

A battle between two hostile kings, each guarded by an imposing array of horse and foot, a death struggle played within a complex set of rules and by preference with pomp and lavish ornament: The game that developed into chess was a fair model of power politics in its birthplace, Central India, sometime during the first millennium. In Sanskrit, it was referred to as *chaturanga,* describing the four arms of contemporary warfare—elephants and chariots, cavalry and infantry—as well as being the root of the word for chess in many languages.

Chess traveled far and fast from its homeland, its rules evolving as it went. So did the style of its pieces, although artisans generally paid some homage to its eastern origins. So, despite his elephant and the howdah he is seated on, the king pictured here was the work not of Indian but of Arab artisans, in ninth-century Basra.

By the eleventh century, chess had reached Sicily and southern Italy, the meeting points of the Muslim and Christian worlds. From there it spread through Europe, already well on its way to becoming a worldwide obsession.

Contacts with the tribal peoples must have been reasonably frequent, for they lived within the empire—in the uplands and the arid plains—not beyond its outer frontiers. No doubt they were the primary source of the banditry that the empire never could put down, for Chola control was strong and effective only in the valleys. Even there, uncultivated land remained, often available for anyone who chose to clear it: Villagers faced with excessive tax demands, rather than risk the cumbersome and uncertain process of appeal through the fragile imperial bureaucracy, would often simply gather their animals and families and move elsewhere.

In that sense, as in many others, the empire was open and fluid, not closed and static. And as it gradually declined from the peak it attained in the years of Rajendra's rule, it did not crumble dramatically into ruin. Rather it changed; the channels of the Kaveri might be fixed in the earth, but the channels by which power and revenue flowed in the network of empire were not, and they could be rearranged.

Back in Shangam times, Karikala himself, it was said, had chosen a tiger as the Chola emblem. It was an appropriate symbol for a predatory, conquering dynasty. But there is a more fitting image for the empire of the Cholas as it had developed, in all its self-regenerating diffuseness, by the eleventh century. It is Shiva himself, in the guise of Nataraja the cosmic dancer. It was a form beloved by Chola sculptors, both in stone and bronze: dancing Shiva, turning within a ring of fire that is the circle of the world, which contains him and which he steps beyond.

In most representations, the god has four hands. One holds the drum whose beating is the rhythm of life. One holds the flame that destroys and regenerates. One hand offers its palm in reassurance; but the fourth is held in an eloquent gesture of

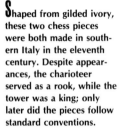

Shaped from gilded ivory, these two chess pieces were both made in southern Italy in the eleventh century. Despite appearances, the charioteer served as a rook, while the tower was a king; only later did the pieces follow standard conventions.

carelessness. Beneath his feet a crushed titan shows that Shiva is dancing upon the bodies of the dead; yet his face, despite the whirling hair that tells of the dance's terrifying speed, smiles with absolute serenity. The world dies and is reborn in an endless cycle of pain and joy. Only the dancer is constant.

Rajendra died in 1044; in the Chola way his son Rajadhiraja had years of experience as coruling prince. There was no significant change in the empire, although Ceylon was gradually abandoned. The boundaries of the empire recoiled a little here, edged forward there; some vassals were strong enough to keep more revenue, and others had to settle for less. After Rajadhiraja came his son and his son's son, a long line of names to be inscribed on temple walls—Kulottunga and Vikrama, Rajaraja and Rajendra, II and III—prefaced by a telling of their mighty deeds. Gradually, the revenues slipped away. Border provinces refused to offer even token allegiance. Trade flourished, although sometimes it chose a different route, and merchants paid tolls to potentates who had at one time ranked far below the Cholas in importance. In the south, the Pāndya dynasty, an old Chola rival, grew strong in the ancient city of Madurai. In the thirteenth century, people still talked of a Chola empire. In the fourteenth century, they did not.

Yet the cycle of southern Indian life went on little changed. In 1300, as Europeans reckoned years, a Muslim sultan armed with fire and sword brought his faith to the Hindu south. But his empire barely survived its creator. Local Hindu rulers reasserted their independence, and the life of the common people continued as it had always done. By the banks of the Kaveri the patient buffalo still plowed the paddy fields, and the rice crop grew. Shiva danced.

Carved from walrus tusks, the king, queen, and bishop from this twelfth-century Scandinavian chess set have a brooding air to match their land's stern climate. The bishop's crook and miter are an early example of Christian imagery in the game.

1000-1010	1010-1020	1020-1030	1030-1040	1040-1050

CHINA

1000-1010: After an inconclusive war with the Khitan people to the north, the Song rulers of China agree to pay the Khitan an annual tribute (1004).

1030-1040: Li Yuanhao, ruler of the Tibetan-speaking Tangut people, launches an attack on northwest China (1038).

1040-1050: A Chinese artisan named Bi Sheng invents movable-type printing (c. 1042).

The Song administrator Fan Zhongyan introduces a ten-p program of bureaucratic, mi tary, and land reforms (1044

After six years of border wa fare, China agrees to pay an tribute to the Tanguts (1044

THE MIDDLE EAST

1030-1040: Seljuk Turks under the leadership of Tughril-Beg seize the Ghaznavid city of Merv (1037).

1040-1050: The Seljuks defeat the Ghaz vids at the Battle of Dandan (1040).

Tughril-Beg takes Isfahan an makes himself master of Ira (1043).

Omar Khayyam, Persian poe and mathematician, is born (1048).

WESTERN EUROPE

1010-1020: The Danish king Cnut succeeds to the English throne, uniting Denmark, Norway, and England into a North Sea empire (1016).

The first Norman knights see active service in southern Italy (1017).

1020-1030: Robert I inherits the dukedom of Normandy (1028).

1030-1040: Rainulf becomes the first Norman to win a fief in Italy (1030).

Robert I dies, and the eight-year-old William becomes duke of Normandy (1035).

Cnut's death leads to the break-up of his empire (1035).

1040-1050: At the Abbey of Bec in Normandy, a celebrated sch is founded that will draw sc ars from all over Europe (10

Emperor Henry III initiates t reform of the papacy with th synods of Sutri and Rome (1

Duke William defeats rebell barons at the battle of Val-è Dunes, confirming his hold Normandy (1047).

RUSSIA AND EASTERN EUROPE

1000-1010: Hungary converts to Christianity (1000 on).

Grand Prince Vladimir continues to enforce the Christianization of Kievan Russia (1000 on).

1010-1020: Grand Prince Vladimir dies, leaving a disputed succession to the Kievan throne (1015).

The Byzantine warrior-emperor Basil II completes the conquest of Bulgaria (1018).

1020-1030: Basil II dies (1025).

1030-1040: Yaroslav the Wise emerges as undisputed ruler of Kievan Russia (1035).

The Church of Saint Sophia is completed in Kiev (1037).

INDIA

1000-1010: Rajaraja, ruler of southern India's Chola empire, invades Ceylon and destroys its capital, Anuradhapura (1000).

Rajaraja's son Rajendra invades the Deccan (1007).

Mahmud of Ghazni, the Turkish ruler of an Islamic empire based in Afghanistan, defeats a coalition of North Indian Hindu rulers at Peshawar (1008).

1010-1020: On the death of his father, Rajendra succeeds as Chola king (1014).

The forces of Mahmud of Ghazni pillage the sacred city of Muttra in northern India (1018).

1020-1030: Rajendra sends a Chola expeditionary force to Bengal (1021).

1030-1040: Rajendra launches a seaborne assault on the Shrivijaya empire in southern Malaya and Sumatra (1030).

1040-1050: The Chola king Rajendra di (1044).

TimeFrame AD 1000-1100

Sima Guang completes his *Mirror for the Art of Government*—a history of China from 403 BC to AD 959 (1084).

The death of Emperor Shenzong, the patron of Wang Anshi, causes the abandonment of his New Policies (1086).

ong astronomers observe the upernova that creates the Crab ebula (1054).

The reforming minister Wang Anshi accedes to power (1069).

The philosopher Chou Tun-i, the man responsible for laying the groundwork of neo-Confucianism, dies (1073).

Su Song, a Song astronomer, designs a celebrated water clock (1088).

Attaining his majority, the young emperor Zhezong puts the reformers back in power (1093).

Alp Arslan defeats the Byzantine emperor Romanus Diogenes at the Battle of Manzikert (1071).

Alp Arslan is stabbed to death in central Asia (1072).

Hasan-i Sabbah, the "Old Man of the Mountains," founds the Assassin sect in Persia (1090).

The Assassins murder the vizier Nizam al-Mulk (1092).

Tughril-Beg dies (1063), to be succeeded by Alp Arslan.

Alp Arslan marches on Byzantine Armenia, sacking the capital, Ani (1064).

The Seljuks capture Jerusalem from the Fatimids (1076).

Sulayman proclaims himself the first sultan of Rum (Rome) in former Byzantine lands (1078).

The troops of the First Crusade defeat the sultan of Rum at Nicaea and Dorylaeum (1097).

ughril-Beg enters Baghdad and appointed sultan by the caliph 055).

Jerusalem falls to the Crusaders (1099).

---

he Normans defeat and capture Pope Leo IX at Civitate 1053).

he pope and the patriarch of Constantinople anathematize ne another, finalizing the chism between the Roman and Greek churches (1054).

ope Nicholas II institutes the College of Cardinals to ensure ree papal elections (1059).

Norman forces under Robert Guiscard complete the conquest of Calabria and Apulia (1060).

Robert Guiscard invades Sicily (1061).

Harold II of England defeats a Norwegian invasion force at Stamford Bridge but is then defeated and killed by William of Normandy at Hastings (1066).

The defeat of Hereward the Wake marks the end of armed resistance to William in England (1072).

The Investiture Contest pits the German emperor Henry IV against Pope Gregory VII (1075).

Temporarily defeated, Henry does penance to Gregory at Canossa (1077).

Robert Guiscard invades the Balkans and defeats the Byzantine emperor Alexius I at the battle of Durazzo (1081).

Gregory VII dies in exile in southern Italy (1085).

The *Domesday Book,* a survey of land tenure in England, is completed (1087).

King William I dies (1087).

The Normans complete the conquest of Sicily (1091).

At the Council of Clermont, Pope Urban II inspires the First Crusade (1095).

---

he death of Yaroslav the Wise eads to a division of the Kievan ealm and renewed civil strife 1054).

Romanus Diogenes accedes to the Byzantine throne (1067).

Romanus Diogenes is deposed by his stepson, Michael VII (1071).

---

he Hindu philosopher Rama-uja writes of the importance of devotional worship (c. 1050).

Kulottunga I of Vengi ascends the Chola throne (1070).

Rampala, the last great Pala king of Bengal, is born (1077).

ACKNOWLEDGMENTS

The following materials have been reprinted with the kind permission of the publishers: Page 25: "Question . . .," and "The minister . . .," quoted in *Government Education and Examinations in Sung China,* by Thomas H. C. Lee, New York: St. Martin's Press, 1985. Page 31: "At first . . .," poem by Su Shi, "On Reading the Poetry of Meng Chiao (751-814)," from *China's Imperial Past,* by Charles O. Hucker, Stanford: Stanford University Press, 1975. Page 49: "It is unwise . . .," quoted in *The Chasnavids,* by C. E. Bosworth, Edinburgh: Edinburgh University Press, 1963. Page 51: "If I appoint . . .," quoted in *Turkestan Down to the Mongol Invasion,* by W. Barthold, Cambridge: The E. J. W. Gibb Memorial Trust, 1977. Page 123: "Upon his expeditions . . .," quoted in *Kievan Russia,* by George Vernadsky, Vol. 2, *The History of Russia,* New Haven: Yale University Press, 1959. Page 148: "When you see . . .," quoted in *The Colas,* by K. A. Nilakanta Sastri, Madras: University of Madras, 1955.

The editors also wish to thank the following individuals and institutions for their valuable assistance in the preparation of this volume:
England: Cambridge—Christel M. Kessler; Joseph Needham, Needham Research Institute; Colin Ronan, Needham Research Institute. Leighton Buzzard—Richard Gem. London—Sarah Barter Bailey, Royal Armouries, H. M. Tower of London; Richard Blurton, Department of Oriental Antiquities, British Museum; Mike Brown; Liz Carmichael, Museum of Mankind; Marie-Louise Collard; Nikolai Dejevsky; Reginald Fish, Zoological Society of London; Mark Karras; Eric Kentley, National Maritime Museum; Fred Lake; Edward McEwan; Thom Richardson, Royal Armouries, H. M. Tower of London; Brian A. Tremain, Photographic Services, British Museum; B. D. Turner, King's College, University of London; Professor Roderick Whitfield, Percival David Foundation, University of London; Jim Wiggins. Loughborough—

David Nicolle. Manchester—Wendy Hopkinson, Simon Archery Foundation. Oxford—Linda Proud; Mary Tregear, Department of Eastern Art, Ashmolean Museum. Richmond, Surrey—Barbara Hicks. York—Penelope Walton.
France: Paris—François Avril, Curateur, Département des Manuscrits, Bibliothèque Nationale; Catherine Bélanger, Chargée des Relations Extérieures du Musée du Louvre; Béatrice Coti, Directrice du Service Iconographique, Éditions Mazenod; Antoinette Decaudin, Documentaliste, Département des Antiquités Orientales, Musée du Louvre.
India: Madras—K. Krishna Murthy, Archaeological Survey of India. New Delhi—Arti Ahluwalia; Deepak Puri; K. K. Sharma. Tanjore—Krishnaji Raje Mahadik.
Scotland: Edinburgh—J. D. Latham, Edinburgh University.
U.S.A.: New York: New York City—Katharine R. Brown, Department of Medieval Art, Metropolitan Museum of Art. Washington, D.C.—Mrs. Alfred Friendly.

PICTURE CREDITS

BIBLIOGRAPHY

BOOKS

Almgren, Bertil, *The Viking.* Gothenburg, Sweden: A. B. Nordbok, 1975.

Amiranashvili, Shalva, *Medieval Georgian Enamels of Russia.* New York: Harry N. Abrams Inc., 1964.

Ars Orientalis: The Arts of Islam and the East. Vol. 3. Washington, D.C.: Smithsonian Institution, 1959.

The Arts of Islam. London: Arts Council of Great Britain, 1976.

Auty, Robert, and Dimitri Obolensky, eds., *An Introduction to Russian History.* Cambridge: Cambridge University Press, 1976.

Baker, Christopher John, *An Indian Rural Economy.* Oxford: Clarendon Press, 1984.

Baker, Timothy, *The Normans.* London: Cassell, 1966.

Barley, M. W., ed., *European Towns: Their Archaeology and Early History.* San Diego: San Diego Academic Press, 1977.

Barraclough, Geoffrey, *The Medieval Papacy.* London: Thames & Hudson, 1968.

Bartebev, I., *North Russian Architecture.* Moscow: Progress Publishers, 1972.

Basham, A. L., *A Cultural History of India.* Oxford: Clarendon Press, 1975.

Beeler, J. H., *Warfare in England 1066-1189.* Ithaca: Cornell University Press, 1966.

Bing, Li Ung, *Outlines of Chinese History.* Shanghai: The Commercial Press, no date.

Birnbaum, Henrik, *Lord Novgorod the Great.* Los Angeles: U.C.L.A. Slavic Studies, 1981.

Blair, Claude, *European Armour c. 1066 to c. 1700.* London: Batsford, 1958.

Blum, Jerome, *Lord and Peasant in Russia.* Princeton: Princeton University Press, 1961.

Blunden, Caroline, and Mark Elvin, *Cultural Atlas of China.* Oxford: Phaidon, 1983.

Bosworth, C. E., *The Ghaznavids.* Edinburgh: Edinburgh University Press, 1963.

Braunfels, Wolfgang, *Monasteries of Western Europe.* London: Thames & Hudson, 1972.

Briggs, Martin S., *Muhammadan Architecture.* Oxford: Clarendon Press, 1924.

Brown, R. Allen, *The Normans.* Woodbridge, England: The Boydell Press, 1984.

Cahen, Claude, *Pre-Ottoman Turkey.* London: Sidgwick & Jackson, 1968.

Caiger-Smith, Alan, *Lustre Pottery.* London: Faber & Faber, 1985.

Cassady, Richard F., *The Norman Achievement.* London: Sidgwick & Jackson, 1986.

Chang, K. C., ed., *Food in Chinese Culture.* New Haven: Yale University Press, 1979.

Charlton, John, ed., *The Tower of London.* London: H. M. Stationery Office, 1978.

Chaudhuri, K. N., *Trade and Civilisation in the Indian Ocean.* Cambridge: Cambridge University Press, 1985.

Chirovsky, Nicholas L., *A History of the Russian Empire.* London: Peter Owen, 1973.

Christie, Grace, *Samplers and Stitches.* London: B. T. Batsford, 1985.

Clayr, Alasdair, *The Heart of the Dragon.* London: Collins / Harvill, 1984.

Coe, Michael D., *The Maya.* Harmondsworth, Middlesex, England: Penguin Books, 1971.

Collon-Gevaert, Suzanne, Jean Lejeune, and Jacques Stiennon, *A Treasury of Romanesque Art.* London: Phaidon, 1972.

Conant, Kenneth John:
Carolingian and Romanesque Architecture. Harmondsworth, Middlesex, England: Penguin Books, 1959.
Cluny: Les Églises et la Maison du Chef d'Ordre. Cambridge, Mass.: The Medieval Academy of America, 1968.

Craven, R. C., *Indian Art.* London: Thames & Hudson, 1976.

Creswell, K. A. C., *Muslim Architecture of Egypt.* Vol. 1. Oxford: Oxford University Press, 1959.

Cross, S. H., and O. P. Sherbowitz-Wetzor, eds. and transls., *The Russian Primary Chronicle.* Cambridge, Mass.: Medieval Academy of America, 1953.

Curtis, Edmund, *Roger of Sicily.* London: G. P. Putnam's Sons, 1912.

Daumas, Maurice, *A History of Technology and Invention.* Vol. 1. London: John Murray, 1980.

Davidson, H. R. Ellis, *The Viking Road to Byzantium.* London: George Allen & Unwin, 1916.

Davis, R. H. C., *The Normans and Their Myth.* London: Thames & Hudson, 1976.

Davis, Richard L., *Court and Family in Sung China, 960-1279.* Durham, N.C.: Duke University Press, 1986.

Dejevsky, Nikolai, "Novgorod: The Origins of a Russian Town." In *European Towns: Their Archaeology and Early History,* ed. by Maurice Willmore Barley. London: Academic Press, 1977.

De Landa, Diego, *Landa's Relación de las Cosas Yucatan.* Ed. by Alfred M. Tozzer. New York: AMS Press, 1941.

Deloche, Jean, *La Circulation en Inde avant la Révolution des Transports.* Vol. 2. Paris: École Française d'Extrême Orient, 1980.

Deschamps, Paul, *French Sculpture of the Romanesque Period.* New York: Harcourt, 1930.

Dmytryshyn, Basil, *Medieval Russia.* Hinsdale, Ill.: The Dryden Press, 1972.

Douglas, David C.:
The Norman Achievement. London: Eyre & Spottiswoode, 1969.
William the Conqueror. London: Eyre & Spottiswoode, 1964.

Dunaev, Mikhail, and Feliks Razumovsky, *Novgorod: A Guide.* Moscow: Raduga Publishers, 1984.

Eberhard, Wolfram, *A History of China.* London: Routledge & Kegan Paul, 1950.

Eck, Diana L., *Darsan: Seeing the Divine Image in India.* Chambersburg, Pa.: Anima Publications, 1985.

Edgerton, Franklin, *The Elephant Lore of the Hindus.* New Haven: Yale University Press, 1931.

Edwardes, Michael, *Indian Temples and Palaces.* London: Paul Hamlyn, 1969.

Elgood, Robert, *Islamic Arms and Armour.* London: Scolar Press, 1979.

Evans, Joan:
Monastic Life at Cluny. London: Oxford University Press, 1931.
The Romanesque Architecture of the Order of Cluny. Cambridge: Cambridge University Press, 1938.

Fedotov, G. P., *The Russian Religious Mind.* Cambridge, Mass.: Harvard University Press, 1966.

Fennell, John, and Antony Stokes, *Early Russian Literature.* London: Faber & Faber, 1974.

Fergusson, James, *History of Indian and Eastern Architecture.* London: John Murray, 1910.

Foote, Peter, and David M. Wilson, *The Viking Achievement.* London: Sidgwick & Jackson, 1970.

Foreville, Raymonde, ed. and transl., *Guillaume de Poitier.* Paris: Société d'Édition 'Les Belles Lettres,' 1952.

Fossati, Gildo, *Monuments of Civilisation: China.* Transl. by Bruce Penman. London: New English Library, 1983.

Friendly, Alfred, *The Dreadful Day.* London: Hutchinson, 1981.

Gantner, Joseph, and Marcel Pobé, *Romanesque Art in France.* London: Thames & Hudson, 1956.

Gernet, Jacques:
Daily Life in China. Stanford, Calif.: Stanford University Press, 1962.
A History of Chinese Civilization. Cambridge: Cambridge University Press, 1982.

Gimbutas, Marija, *The Slavs.* London: Thames & Hudson, 1971.

Gippenreiter, V., E. Gordienko, and S. Yamshchikov, *Novgorod.* Moscow: Planeta Publishers, 1976.

Grabar, Andrei N., *Early Medieval Painting.* Lausanne, Switzerland: Skira, 1957.

Graham-Campbell, J. A., and Dafydd Kidd, *The Vikings.* London: British Museum Publications, 1980.

Grousset, René, *The Rise and Splendour of the Chinese Empire.* London: Geoffrey Bles, 1953.

Grover, Satish, *The Architecture of India.* Sahibabad, India: Vikas Publishing, 1980.

Grube, Ernst J., *Islamic Pottery.* London: Faber & Faber, 1976.

Haeger, John Winthrop, ed., *Crisis and Prosperity in Sung China.* Tucson: University of Arizona Press, 1975.

Hall, Kenneth R.:
Maritime Development and State Development in Early Southeast Asia. Honolulu: University of Hawaii Press, 1985.
Trade and Statecraft in the Age of the Colas. New Delhi: Abhinav Publications, 1980.

Hamilton, George Heard, *The Art and Architecture of Russia.* Harmondsworth, Middlesex, England: Penguin Books, 1983.

Hammond, Norman, *Ancient Maya Civilisation.* Cambridge: Cambridge University Press, 1982.

Harrow, Leonard, and Peter Lamborn Wilson, *Science and Technology in Islam.* London: Crescent Moon Press, 1976.

al-Hassan, Ahmed, and Donald R. Hill, *Islamic Technology: An Illustrated History.* Cambridge: Cambridge University Press, 1986.

Hayes, John R., ed., *The Genius of Arab Civilisation.* London: Phaidon, 1978.

Hearn, M. F., *Romanesque Sculpture.* Oxford: Phaidon, 1981.

Hinde, Thomas, *The Domesday Book.* London: Hutchinson, 1985.

Hitti, Philip K., *History of the Arabs.* London: Macmillan, 1970.

Hoag, John D., *Islamic Architecture.* New York: Harry N. Abrams Inc., 1977.

Holt, P. M., *The Age of the Crusades.* London: Longmans, 1986.

Hook, Brian, ed., *The Cambridge History of China.* Cambridge: Cambridge University Press, 1982.

Hornell, James, "The Origins and Ethnological Significance of Indian Boat Design." In *Memoirs of the Asiatic Society of Bengal.* Calcutta: The Asiatic Society of Bengal, 1923.

Hornell, James, *Water Transport.* Newton Abbot, England: David and Charles, 1970.

Hoyle, Fred, *Astronomy.* London: Macdonald, 1962.

Hucker, Charles O., *China's Imperial Past.* Stanford, Calif.: Stanford University Press, 1975.

Hunt, Noreen, *Cluny under Saint Hugh.* London: Edward Arnold, 1967.

Huyghe, René, ed., *Larousse Encyclopaedia of Byzantine and Medieval Art.* London: Paul Hamlyn, 1968.

Jenyns, R. Soame, and William Watson, *Chinese Art.* London: Oldbourne Press, 1963.

Jones, Gwyn, *A History of the Vikings.* Oxford: Oxford University Press, 1968.

Karger, M., *Novgorod the Great.* Moscow: Progress Publishers, 1973.

Keay, John, *India Discovered.* Leicester, England: Windward, 1981.

Kerner, Robert J., *The Urge to the Sea.* New York: Russell & Russell, 1971.

Khayyam, Omar, *The Ruba'iyat of Omar Khayyam.* Ed. by Peter Avery and John Heath-Stubbs. Harmondsworth, Middlesex, England: Penguin Books, 1981.

Kirkby, Michael H., *The Vikings.* Oxford: E. P. Dutton, 1977.

Kitzinger, Ernst, *Early Medieval Art.* London: Trustees of the British Museum, 1955.

Klopsteg, Paul E., *Turkish Archery and the Composite Bow.* Evanston, Ill.: Privately published, 1934.

Knowles, David, *Christian Monasticism.* London: Weidenfeld & Nicolson, 1969.

Kochan, Lionel, and Richard Abraham, *The Making of Modern Russia.* London: Jonathan Cape, 1962.

Kramisch, Stella, *The Hindu Temple.* Calcutta: University of Calcutta, 1946.

Latham, J. D., and W. F. Paterson, *Saracen Archery: An English Version of a Mameluke Work on Archery c. 1368.* London: The Holland Press, 1970.

Lee, Thomas H. C., *Government Education and Examinations in Sung China.* New York: St. Martin's Press, 1985.

Lindsay, Jack, *The Normans and Their World.* London: Hart-Davis, MacGibbon Ltd., 1974.

Lovell, Hin-Cheung, *Illustrated Catalogue of Ting Yao and Related White Wares.* London: School of Oriental and African Studies, 1964.

Macdonald, John, *Great Battlefields of the World.* London: Michael Joseph, 1984.

Maudslay, Alfred, *Archaeology.* London: R. H. Porter and Dulau, 1889-1902.

Medley, Margaret:
The Chinese Potter. Oxford: Phaidon, 1980.
Illustrated Catalogue of Ting and Allied Wares. London: School of Oriental and African Studies, 1980.

Mehta, Rustam J., *Masterpieces of Indian Bronzes.* Bombay: D. B. Traporevala Sons, 1971.

Meyendorff, John, *Byzantium and the Rise of Russia.* Cambridge: Cambridge University Press, 1981.

Mirsky, D. S., *Russia: A Social History.* London: Cresset Press, 1931.

Mirsky, Jeanette, *Houses of God.* London: Constable, 1965.

Moravcsik, Gyula, ed., *Constantine Porphyrogenitus de Administrando Imperio.* Transl. by R. J. H. Jenkins. Harvard: Trustees for Harvard University, 1967.

Needham, Joseph, *Science and Civilisation in China.* Vol. 4 Part 1 and Vol. 5 Part 1. Cambridge: Cambridge University Press, 1985.

Needham, Joseph, et al., *Heavenly Clockwork.* Cambridge: Antiquarian Horological Society, 1960.

Norwich, John Julius, *The Normans in the South.* London: Longmans, 1967.

Oman, G. W. C., *A History of the Art of War in the Middle Ages.* London: Methuen and Co., 1924.

Oursel, Raymond, *Living Architecture: Romanesque.* London: Oldbourne, 1967.

Paskiewicz, Henryk, *The Making of the Russian Nation.* London: Darton, Longman & Todd, 1963.

Philon, Helen, *Early Islamic Ceramics.* London: Islamic Art Publications, 1980.

Pipes, Richard, *Russia under the Old Regime.* London: Weidenfeld & Nicolson, 1974.

Pirenne, Jacques, *The Tides of History.* Vol. 2. London: George Allen & Unwin, 1963.

Portal, Roger, *The Slavs.* London: Weidenfeld & Nicolson, 1969.

Postan, M. M., ed., *The Cambridge Economic History of Europe.* Vol. 1. Cambridge: Cambridge University Press, 1966.

Prakash, Vidya, *Khajuraho.* Bombay: D. B. Taraporevala Sons, 1967.

Rice, David Talbot, *Islamic Art.* London: Thames & Hudson, 1986.

Rice, Tamara Talbot:
A Concise History of Russian Art. London: Thames & Hudson, 1963.
The Seljuks in Asia Minor. London: Thames & Hudson, 1961.

Riddell, Sheila, *Dated Chinese Antiquities.* London: Faber & Faber, 1979.

Ronan, Colin, *Cambridge Illustrated History of the World's Science.* Cambridge: Cambridge University Press, 1983.

Rybakov, B. A., *Russian Applied Art of the Tenth-Thirteenth Centuries.* Leningrad: Aurora Art Publishers, 1971.

Sanderson, Ivan T., *The Dynasty of Abu.* London: Cassell, 1983.

Sarton, George, *Introduction to the History of Science.* Vol. 1. Washington, D.C.: Carnegie Institution, 1927.

Sastri, K. A. Nilakanta, *The Colas.* Madras: University of Madras, 1955.

Saunders, J. J., *A History of Medieval Islam.* London: Routledge & Kegan Paul, 1972.

Searle, Eleanor, ed. and transl., *The Chronicle of Battle Abbey.* Oxford: Clarendon Press, 1980.

Shebbeare, E. O., *Soondar Mooni.* London: Gollancz, 1958.

Shiba, Yoshinobu, *Commerce and Society in Sung China.* Transl. by Mark Elvin. Ann Arbor, Mich.: University of Michigan Center for Chinese Studies, 1970.

Sickman, Laurence, and Alexander Soper, *The Art and Architecture of China.* Harmondsworth, Middlesex, England: Penguin Books, 1968.

Singer, Charles, A. R. Hall, and E. J. Holmyard, *History of Technology.* Vol. 2. Oxford: Clarendon Press, 1956.

Sircar, Dines Chandra, *Select Inscriptions Bearing on Indian History and Civilization.* Vol. 2. Delhi: Motilal Banarsidass, 1983.

Smith, Bradley, and Wan-go Weng, *China: A History in Art.* London: Studio Vista, 1973.

Smith, Denis Mack, *A History of Sicily.* Vol. 2. London: Chatto & Windus, 1968.

Smith, R. E. F., *The Origins of Farming in Russia.* Paris: Mouton and Co., 1959.

Sourdel, D., and J. Sourdel, *La Civilisation de l'Islam Classique.* Paris: Arthaud, 1976.

Southern, R. W., *The Making of the Middle Ages.* London: The Cresset Library, 1987.

Ssu-ch'eng, Liang, *The Pictorial History of Chinese Architecture.* Ed. by Wilma Fairbank. Cambridge, Mass.: Massachusetts Institute of Technology, 1984.

Stein, Burton, *Peasant State and Society in Medieval South India.* Delhi: Oxford University Press, 1980.

Steinhardt, Nancy Shatzman, et al., *Chinese Traditional Architecture.* New York: China Institute in America, 1984.

Stenton, Frank, ed., *The Bayeux Tapestry.* London: Phaidon, 1957.

Stierlin, H., *Living Architecture: Mayan.* Fribourg: Office du Livre, 1964.

Swarzenski, Hanns, *Monuments of Romanesque Art.* London: Faber & Faber, 1954.

Taralon, Jean, *L'Abbaye de Jumièges.* Paris: La Caisse Nationale des Monuments Historiques et des Sites, 1979.

Taton, René, ed., *Ancient and Medieval Science from the Beginning to AD 1450.* Vol. 1 of *A General History of the Sciences.* London: Thames & Hudson, 1964.

Tellenbach, Gerd, *Church, State and Christian Society at the Time of the Investiture Contest.* Transl. by R. F. Bennett. Oxford: Basil Blackwell, 1959.

Temple, Elzbieta, *Anglo-Saxon Manuscripts.* London: Harvey Miller, 1976.

Temple, Robert K. G., *China: Land of Discovery.* Wellingborough, England: Patrick Stephens, 1986.

Thorn, Frank, and Caroline Thorn, *Domesday Book 21: Northamptonshire.* Chichester, England: Phillimore, 1979.

Tikhomirov, M., *The Towns of Ancient Rus.* Moscow: Foreign Language Publishing House, 1959.

Vana, Zdenek, *World of the Ancient Slavs.* Transl. by Till Gottheinerova. Detroit: Wayne State University Press, 1984.

Vernadsky, George:
Kievan Russia. Vol. 2 of *The History of Russia.* New Haven: Yale University Press, 1973.
Medieval Russian Laws. Columbia: Columbia University Press, 1947.
The Origins of Russia. Westport: Greenwood Press, 1975.

Virey, Jean, *L'Abbaye de Cluny.* Paris: Henri Laurens, 1921.

Volkoff, Vladimir, *Vladimir the Russian Viking.* London: Honeyglen Publishing, 1984.

Vryonis, S., *Byzantium: Its Internal History and Relations with the Muslim World.* London: Variorum, 1971.

Waern, Cecilia, *Medieval Sicily.* London: Duckworth, 1910.

Warner, Philip, *Sieges of the Middle Ages.* London: G. Bell and Sons, 1968.

Watson, William, *The Art of Dynastic China.* London: Thames & Hudson, 1981.

Weng, Wan-go, *The Palace Museum: Peking.* London: Orbis Publishing, 1982.

Wichmann, Hans, and Siegfried Wichmann, *Chess.* London: Paul Hamlyn, 1964.

Wiet, Gaston, *The Mosques of Cairo.* Paris: Librairie Hachette, 1966.

Williams, C. A. S., *Outlines of Chinese Symbolism and Art Motives.* Shanghai: Kelly & Walsh, 1932.

Zarnecki, George, *The Art of the Medieval World.* New York: Henry C. Abrams, 1975.

Zwalf, Wladimir, *Buddhism: Art and Faith.* London: British Museum Publications, 1985.

PERIODICALS

Bunt, Cyril G. E., "Russian Art." *The Studio* (London), 1946.

Graham, Rose, and A. W. Clapham, "The Monastery of Cluny 910-1155." *Archaelogia* (London), Vol. 80, 1930.

Pryor, J. H., "The Transportation of Horses by Sea during the Era of the Crusades." *The Mariner's Mirror* (London), Vol. 68, 1982.

INDEX